FINANCIAL
SECRETS
REVEALED

Collective wisdom
from business gurus,
financial geniuses and
everyday heroes

AMANDA CASSAR

General investment advice warning

The material contained in this publication is intended to provide a general commentary only and is not specific or personal financial advice. This publication is no substitute for personal financial advice and does not take into account any individual person's specific situation, goals or needs.

If you are considering acquiring a financial product, ensure you always obtain a Product Disclosure Statement and consider its contents before making any decisions.

This book interviews people from various countries with rules and taxation laws that differ. The anecdotes and opinions do not constitute advice.

Always consider any information in light of your own personal circumstances, place of residence, needs and objectives and consult a licensed financial adviser before taking any action.

Interview disclaimer

The stories in this publication have been told to me by the persons being interviewed and are their personal perceptions, recollections and ideas. Opinions expressed do not necessarily reflect those of the author, and personal stories have not been reviewed or researched for accuracy.

Dedication

Thank you to my friends, family and colleagues for your ongoing love, support and inspiration.

About the author

Amanda is a writer, reader, blogger, dreamer, traveller, wife, mother, friend, aunty, scuba diver, occasional mountain climber and weekend motorbike rider, who truly believes that life is an adventure that needs to be lived.

Amanda is a qualified financial adviser based on the Gold Coast in Queensland, Australia. She holds a master of financial planning along with specialist designations Accredited Aged Care Professional and SMSF Specialist Adviser.

She is a member of the Association of Financial Advisers (AFA), the Financial Planning Association (FPA), the Self Managed Super Fund Association (SMSFA) and a qualifying member of the international group the Million Dollar Round Table (MDRT). Amanda has also been voted as one of the Financial Standard Power50 Most Influential Advisers in Australia.

Her businesses Wealth Planning Partners and Trusted Aged Care Services are run from her office in Robina, Queensland. She is also soon to launch FinEdge Financial Education, assisting with financial literacy in the online world.

Amanda is married with two adult children.

Acknowledgements

I'd like to say a special thank you to everyone who has collaborated with me on this book – whether in my own time zone or across borders, both national and international. Thank you so much for coming together with me to share your unique insights and individual financial journeys. I know your personal experiences will be welcomed by many.

Everyone interviewed in this book gave of their own time freely and willingly, with no 'cash for comment', and I couldn't be more grateful to them for entrusting me with their personal histories, stories, experiences and ideas on money, and for sharing their journeys with me. You're all brave and bold and I appreciate you allowing me to pass on your collective wisdom.

A special thanks to Emma Isaacs and the amazing tribe of Business Chicks for their brilliant spirit and guiding hand to help lift each other up. Finding your tribe was a wonderful gift and being a part of it is an honour and a privilege.

Thanks to The Hunger Project for the amazing work you do globally, helping the poorest of the poor to affect their own change, and for the journeys you've provided – from the Leadership and Immersion Program, to meeting and getting to know the inspirational villagers in Africa who shared their stories on rising above poverty in Uganda and Malawi.

And thanks also to Hands Across the Water and to Peter and Claire Baines for allowing me to partner on their Social Venture Program in Thailand and assist with tearing down a home in the Khlong Toei slums and help in the orphanages in Northern Thailand. Meeting Mai Thew and the children was a rare gift I'll forever cherish. I can't wait to return and partner with you again.

Thank you to my team at Wealth Planning Partners, with a special mention to Leanne Brazel – without your support, I could not do what I do each day, month and year. Another special mention must go to Maree Lallensack, the regional manager of my licensee, for her ongoing support and mentoring. You're a total asset to Financial Services Partners and I'm sure they treasure you as much as I do.

Another shout-out to Sharon Cummins for seeing something in me as a rookie adviser and fighting for my place in the profession with her Dealer Group in the dim distant past.

Thanks also to my lifelong friends, Danielle Hann and Louise Marron. Danielle, thanks for proofing my drafts and for your diabolically rigorous editing skills – and also for being the 'other half of my brain' and sharing my journey on this planet longer than most. And thanks to Louise for providing a roof over my head when needed and allowing me to lay some 'spicy kisses' on your gorgeous boys.

And a final thank you to my amazing family, who put up with my hours on the keyboard, at the office, at conferences and just regularly going AWOL to see clients, do speaking gigs and attend multitudes of conferences and workshops.

First published in 2018 by Amanda Cassar

Wealth Planning Partners Pty Ltd (Practice) is a Corporate Authorised Representative of Financial Services Partners Pty Limited (AFSL No. 237590 ABN 15 089 512 587). (Financial Services Partners). Amanda Cassar is an Authorised Representative of Financial Services Partners.

A catalogue record for this book is available from the National Library of Australia.

ISBN: 978-1-925648-54-6

Project management and text design by Michael Hanrahan Publishing
Cover design by Peter Reardon

Photo credits:

Brad Fox: Photo Courtesy of the AFA; Amanda Cassar: Amy Neeson Photography; Emma Isaacs: Brittany Woodford; Ali Hill: Shae Style Photography; Babette Bensoussan: Permission granted; Tina Tower: Love Photography; Tanya Targett: Permission granted; Michelle Hoskin: Permission granted; Susanne Bransgrove: Permission granted; Lea Schodel: Photo Courtesy of the AFA; David Braithwaite: Richard Bass; Doug Bennett: Permission granted; Jenny Brown: Permission granted by Zurich; Erin Truscott: Ray Cash Photography; David Batchelor: Permission granted; Peita Diamantidis: Eden Connell of Zoom in with Eden; Amy Neeson: Angela Hawkey Photography; Amy Neeson and family: Amanda Cassar; Ann-Marie Von Douglas: Amy Neeson Photography; Peter Baines: Wil Horner; Drew Gaffney: Permission granted.

Disclaimer

Contents

Part II: Financial geniuses

Part III: Everyday heroes

Foreword

I am honoured to have been asked by Amanda Cassar to write this foreword.

I first met Amanda in 2007 at a financial advice conference, and it struck me immediately that this red-haired, vibrant, spirited woman was going to make a real difference – come hell or high water.

As a career-changer who had just entered financial advice, I was eager to learn, and I've always believed the best place to learn is from your peers. Amanda was one of these – honest, considered and trustworthy.

This wonderful book brings together many of Amanda's insightful and motivating peers from around the globe, from within financial advice and business ownership, philanthropy and, in part III, from everyday life. There really is something here for all readers, even if it's being able to feel normal about your own experiences with money throughout life – both the good and the bad.

You won't find any get-rich-quick schemes here, but you will find yourself questioning your relationship with money, and that's an issue we all need to confront at some stage in life.

Money is an enabler; it is nothing more or less than that. Amanda's book serves to remind us that the real richness in life comes from making a contribution to others. Success really is centred on what you give, and not what you get.

Amanda and her contributors, through being both open and vulnerable, have each given generously of themselves.

I have great pleasure in recommending *Financial Secrets Revealed* to anyone who is ready to explore being more than a balance sheet, letting go of hang-ups and misconceptions about money, and finding balance across finances, people and values.

Brad Fox

Brad Fox is an industry thought leader in financial services, having led the Association of Financial Advisers Limited (AFA) as President from 2010 to 2012, and then as Chief Executive Officer from 2012 to 2017. This period included influencing government and other stakeholders on the most substantial reforms to financial services legislation in Australia for more than 40 years.

Brad is the Founder and Managing Director at SmartBrave Consulting, and holds directorships with the Pro-Bono Financial Advice Network, Salesian College Sunbury, and two highly regarded Australian financial advice businesses, as well as being a passionate coach of junior Australian Rules Football, father and husband.

Introduction

The working title for this book was *The Best Financial Advice Ever* and that is a pretty big call, I know. But then, I've asked a lot of pretty incredible people for their advice in this book. I've asked amazing men and women who run some incredible companies, both nationally and internationally, for their unique views. I've also asked some financial services geniuses from Australia and around the world for their stories. And I've included some everyday battlers' views on budgeting, finances and advice. I think they're heroes!

Financial advice in Australia and the United Kingdom is only sought by 20 per cent of the population, yet all of us deal with money on a daily basis, no matter where we're based in the world. Before we're even born, we're costing our folks money and, by the time we're ready for our first job, we realise that money is going to be essential for the term of our natural lives. Along with my colleagues, I'd love to increase the percentage of people who seek financial advice, and hope the information in this book helps you understand why.

The big issue in this book

By the time most people leave school, start work and take out their first mortgage, they're wondering why they don't know more about money. Why financial literacy isn't as essential in schools as reading, writing and arithmetic, I'll never understand. I'd love a curriculum that teaches financial literacy from infancy, where money-savvy young adults leave school for university or the workforce, able to navigate a budget, know how the increasingly cashless society works and understand how our retirement systems work.

Fortunately for our sanity, a lot of things do make sense in the world. We can bet that the sun will continue to rise, puppy pictures will keep rocking the internet, goat memes will make us laugh, teens will make stupid mistakes from lack of experience, motivational quotes will continue to rule social media, nothing will ever be better than wine and a good book, and that despite awful setbacks, life truly will go on.

So the big issue in this book - and the issue that really 'sticks in my craw' as a lifetime career financial adviser - is financial literacy. I hope this book provides lessons in finance that we all wish we'd known earlier, and were never taught. Seriously, our lives revolve around the almighty dollar, whether we want them to or not, so we need to know its workings.

Some tell me financial literacy is the responsibility of the parents, but seeing most parents have never been taught the basics and still struggle themselves, them being able to raise financially competent young people is unlikely.

These days, people have plenty of places to turn to if they want to get it together financially - including online and in-person courses, books galore, and myriad websites, budget planning tools, blogs, seminars, conferences and apps. Expert help is available wherever we turn. Sometimes, even good old-fashioned common sense (which isn't really that common anymore) can be the best teacher. All these methods are great and, depending on how you like to learn, something is available that's right up your alley! The trick is finding what works for you.

How our backgrounds shape us

I 'fell' into financial planning when I left school and went to work for a family friend who was a life insurance and superannuation agent. I'd never heard of financial advisers at that stage, and the only finance jobs I knew of were for accountants and economists – neither of which tugged at my career heart strings – yet somehow I ended up an adviser as the industry began its long and slow evolution into a profession (a journey that's still taking place). After talking to a lot of other financial planners, I've realised many of them also became an accidental adviser while following some other career path. And despite the role's more professional status, those leaving school with dreams of becoming a financial adviser are still few and far between (if they exist at all!).

Often we inherit traits and belief patterns from our family, friends and environment. Our religious beliefs are often those of the faith we're 'born into' and then, as we age, we choose whether this is what's in our heart or not. The football team we choose to follow may be as generational as our faith, and the car we drive may be based on what we were told was the best by Dad. Even how we hang the washing out and do the ironing is likely exactly how we were taught. Of course, how you do something may not be how others do it, and sometimes there isn't right or wrong, just different. The values taught to us by our parents can become intrinsic to who we are, or rejected outright as we forge our own paths.

Over the years, I've wondered how all this relates to money – that is, how much our familial beliefs about money shape who we are and what we become, and whether we embrace those ideas consciously, or form our own as we age and change. I've always wanted to know more about how those unspoken financial lessons, the ones set by example, affect us over time and whether we value them or choose our own path. Do these experiences and lessons affect us forever, becoming lifetime limiting beliefs? Do we even understand that we have them? Or at some stage do we sit up and realise that certain ideas no longer resonate and we just don't agree with them or need them anymore? Conversely, were some of them really smart and we realise we've managed to incorporate them and be guided by those rules to this day?

So as I began work on this book, I chose to interview a series of people who are in business - as mentioned, some who own their own businesses or are in the financial services profession, and others who are everyday heroes, going about their lives, trying to make ends meet.

As well as finding out aspects like the best financial advice they've been given and how they've applied it in their lives, I wanted to know a little more about these people's parents and their family lives growing up. I want to find out what lessons were imparted, whether intentionally or not - and whether those lessons still applied.

The coming chapters introduce you to different people from Australia and around the world, and give you a little of their background and family held beliefs about money. I get personal and delve into their lives growing up and their current biographies, and ask about how they do things financially, both personally and in business. I asked the questions I did to see if any patterns emerged, and to uncover whether our 'inherited' ideas were still those we chose to run with as adults or if we made our own choices. And I interviewed men and women from all walks of life, different faiths, countries, beliefs and forms of employment to see what I could discover. I've also included my own story at the start of the book, delving into similar areas in my history as I discuss with the interviewees. This tells you a little more about me and shares my journey as a financial adviser. Only after doing all the interviews did it occur to me how my personal circle includes many amazing business women who've kindly shared their journeys, and I hope you enjoy hearing from them too.

The interviews

This book doesn't have to be read in perfect order. I've broken the interviews into three separate parts, which makes the book pretty easy to pick up and put down wherever you like.

Tips collected from the business gurus (featured in part I) may not interest you, whereas advice from financial professionals (part II) or everyday heroes (part III) might be more of a priority. Alternately, the advice from those in business might be your favourite part – it's completely up to you! Whatever takes your fancy! Read a lot or not much at all. This is an easy book to pick up and just read a little, with each chapter dedicated solely to the person being interviewed at the time.

I'm sure you'll agree that most of the people I've interviewed in part I are pretty amazing, but they probably wouldn't categorise themselves as 'gurus'. They're the sort of people who've decided to take a chance on themselves and unleash their great idea – whether a product or service – onto their communities, nationally, or even the world at large.

If you'd rather jump ahead and see what the financial geniuses (or is that genii?) have to say, that's fine too. These are the people who work in the financial services profession and give clients advice, and I've added a bit of an international flavour with some advisers from the United Kingdom thrown in too.

I've also interviewed a few people who I view as everyday heroes. They're going about their lives making a dollar and making a difference, whether to their own families and communities, or on a global scale.

Most of the people I interviewed have crossed my path over the past few years and left an impact of some sort. Before each interview, I introduce the interviewee and let you know how we met. I then outline the series of questions I asked them and provide their answers – so you get to hear their tips and ideas in their own words. I certainly would have loved to have included many more people and to have heard their stories too, but that's the beauty of this style of interview book – I've already got the next one in mind!

I'm no psychologist – just a nosy financial adviser trying to put two and two together to get four. So at the end of each interview I include the key points I took from the chats. (I've also included there a favourite quote from each of the interviewees.) I hope you enjoy the interviews and my key take-outs and findings.

Getting the most out of this book

I've always known I wanted to write a book, but the last thing I wanted was to be another 'wanky financial adviser' writing a book on how to budget. I'm pretty sure a few of those kinds of books are already out there.

I hope you enjoy this collective wisdom and get some top tips from the incredible people to follow. Hopefully, you'll learn interesting insights from those in business, understand the work that financial planners go through with their clients and take some gems away from the everyday heroes I wrap up the book with.

I hope you will also be able to learn from the individual journeys of each person featured, and the paths on which they've chosen to forge ahead.

> Money, pardon the expression, is like manure. It's not worth a thing unless it's spread around, encouraging young things to grow.
>
> Dolly Levi, *Hello, Dolly!*

My story

'Know your numbers and learn to live within your means.'

@financechicks
@WealthPP
@trustedagedcare

Family life growing up...

I grew up in middle-class Australia, the oldest of three children on Queensland's Gold Coast, a holiday capital in Oz full of theme parks, beaches and spectacular weather. The local schools were walking or riding distance away, and we'd catch up with friends along the way and travel together.

We were only blocks away from the fabulous Coral Sea and most holidays were spent at and around the beach or with my grandparents in rural areas. As I was a pasty white, freckled, redhead kid who could not get a tan among all the surfing babes and boys, bullying was a part of my early primary school journey. But, like they say, what doesn't kill you makes you stronger and the experience has, in turn, engendered in me a burning hatred of injustice and anything that's just 'not fair'.

My father was the main breadwinner in the family, as was still very much the custom in the 1970s. Dad was an insurance agent who specialised in business insurance and commercial cover, house and contents and car insurances. So, yes, I've been around the insurance and finance world since birth, growing up with the jargon of policies, premiums and claims over the dining table. Mum was a qualified hairdresser and so helped out with the finances in between raising the kids. When my parents built their first family home in Palm Beach, it included a small room that could be used as a sewing room or salon, so Mum could continue her home hairdressing for friends and family. The home in Palm Beach was where I grew up and stayed until I got married, just shy of 21. My parents stayed in this home for almost 30 years.

Mum and Dad worked hard for what they had and, like most of their generation, were fairly conservative. Not long after they'd moved into their home, a recession hit and interest rates went as high as 18 per cent. Splurging was not an option and Dad stuck us all to a strict budget.

I actually didn't know you could buy chicken pieces without skin on and bones included, or potatoes that someone else had washed until I started helping out with the groceries. These were luxuries we didn't need to take. I don't remember ever staying in a hotel and rarely did restaurants form a part of our life. A treat was every year or so, driving to Point Danger in Coolangatta with a bucket of KFC for the family to share and chasing seagulls on the windy bluffs that crashed down to the ocean and rocks below. It was definitely a much simpler time.

After high school, I really didn't know what I wanted to do with my life. Teachers told me I was wasting my academic ability by not heading off to university but still I drifted into waitressing, teaching music and doing teacher aide work part time at a local hinterland primary school.

A friend of my father's ran a small life insurance business locally and, when his secretary decided to move to Sydney, he asked if I'd like to start work with him. Like I said, lightning still hadn't struck me on the career front and more regular work sounded good, so I accepted. I was about 18, soon to be engaged and ready to learn.

When I started, we had a hefty 256 computer to run the business, a dot matrix printer and an ancient envelope style filing system. I'm sure that all was a huge investment of around $10,000 back then! Policies had recently become 'unbundled' and the usual name changes and consolidations of insurance companies were well underway by the early 1990s. Legislation was on the horizon, but certainly not impacting how we managed back then. Simply, we felt we left every client better off for meeting with us – and that was without epic fact-finding documents, statements of advice, disclosure documents and all the new and looming consumer facing tools that were still ahead.

So that's a little bit about early experiences. To provide more detail on my background and how this has shaped the person I am today and the way I approach my finances, I've provided answers to the kinds of questions I asked all the interviewees featured in this book. (You can also find out more about me through @financechicks @WealthPP and @trustedagedcare.)

Within three years of starting work, I was married and moved out of home. We pretty much had nothing when my husband and I started off. The elderly people whose former home we were renting sold us some of their furniture quite cheaply because they were moving into a smaller unit, but that was about it. We lived pay cheque to pay cheque, using our limited tax returns for an annual holiday and doing our best to manage a limited budget and make ends meet.

Within two years, I was pregnant and we needed to downsize from the rented home to a unit, get rid of the family dog and change the old cars we owned (circa 1964 and 1974). I returned to part-time work within six weeks of having my son, taking him to work with me. Around 12 months later, we decided we'd expand the family, thinking that the two babies would be nice and close. I then took two years off paid work to be with the kids while my husband ran a lawn mowing run. Times were definitely lean and supplemented by Centrelink payments, but we were happy and busy with our young family. Having said that, I didn't want to keep living so hand to mouth and knew things had to change.

When my daughter was two, I was offered my job back in the planning firm I'd left while on maternity leave and returned to my former role in administration. This time, however, I decided to do it for me. I already knew the work and how the products operated and where they fitted together, and so managed to also study part-time. We were also able by this stage to purchase our first home, with the help of family. This was prior to the introduction of the GST (the goods and services tax – introduced in Australia in 2000), and things were much cheaper.

Over the coming years, I completed my Diploma of Financial Services with Deakin University, and then my advanced diploma, having a little time off before completing my Master of Financial Planning online.

Once qualified to be an adviser, I moved from part-time admin to also looking after clients and starting to supplement our family income with occasional insurance commission or advice fees. When the children started school, I was still able to take time off in the mornings to change the readers, do tuck shop duty and drop off and pick them up. The flexibility was great for the family.

Over time, we built and sold homes, building up equity and are just about to commence our fourth build, which will reduce our debt even further. My business has built substantially over time and I bought out my former employer on his retirement in 2014. If there is one thing constant, however, that's change.

Although I have never faced massive financial disruption, I do know what it's like to live from week to week and have to budget heavily to make ends meet. Starting from a low base financially is fine, but the first thing I had to change to make a difference was my mindset. For some years, I thought it was just 'my circumstances' or outside influences that meant we weren't really well off. It was only when I took complete financial responsibility that things began to turn around for us. I still believe our attitude is the starting point to making changes. Laying blame and making excuses will never help us to forge a new path.

How can financial professionals help?

Legislation changes each annual budget and keeping up with the differences from year to year is a part of the job. Politicians can use retirement savings and products as political footballs and staying up to date is imperative. Changes to how we're able to earn a living can be decided by people who know very little about what we do and how we're actually remunerated and, over time, many advisers have decided that these changes are too hard to keep up with. Yet, seeing the changes daily that advisers make in their clients' lives is still incredibly rewarding. I know that people can be overwhelmed by their financial situation when I meet them, but I know (and love) that I can reduce complexity and take a load off. I know, too, that when things go bad, I'm the one turning up with the insurance cheque to help make ends meet when everyone else has their hand out. I know my colleagues also find this incredibly rewarding.

I know that most of us 'don't know what we don't know', and I love the idea of outsourcing to professionals or experts when needed, and am more than happy to do that myself. The other way a professional can help is to keep you accountable – vital to achieving results.

I still choose to believe some ideas from my parents, and not others. I've forged my own path and truly believe in the value of advice.

I'm certainly not as conservative as my parents and am more prepared to take a well-researched risk. I'm also not as tight and believe in still enjoying life in the now, while being responsible for later on. I'm happy to invest in assets that my parents would have never considered, and that give me pleasure as well as a possible capital gain, like art. But I've also learned a great lesson, and that is to live within your means.

Do I use any financial apps?

I do all my banking via apps. I had bank accounts hacked from a computer I used once, and have never accessed my banking from a desktop since. Thankfully, the hack was reported immediately and the bank covered the transactions for me.

I'm a partner with My Prosperity and offer the use of their app plus coaching to my clients. I also have the ASX app on my phone so I can check stock prices if I need to, and the XE currency converter for when I travel.

My top financial tip

My top tip is live within your means. I don't think it can get any easier or clearer than that. Doing it, however, can be a little trickier and is all about knowing your numbers.

Understanding exactly what is going out of your account for set bills on a weekly or monthly - even annual - basis is vital to managing your finances. Don't worry about what the income is to start with but understand what it costs you to wake up and take a breath each day. Then, bring in the income and work out whether your expenses are above or below your take-home pay. That's when you need to make adjustments to your lifestyle, start an investment portfolio or bring down debt.

What would I like my children to learn about money?

I want my children to know their numbers. My son left trade school and wanted to be a mechanic, but after a couple of years in an apprenticeship left that and came and worked with me. He's now completed his Advanced Diploma in Financial Planning and has started advising, so hopefully he's learned a few things along the way. He's also moved out of home and living with his partner so he's been learning firsthand about finances and makes sure saving is still a priority.

My daughter is a qualified make-up artist, but is struggling to find work, so without any income a budget is a little difficult for her.

What's really important to me is that they're happy and healthy and understand how to make ends meet.

Do I stick with a family budget?

Yes. Each year as a bare minimum, I use the ASIC MoneySmart website and run our family budget. I also do a personal budget based on my portion of the family's expenses. Understanding exactly what comes out of the set pay I choose to take from my business makes life a lot easier. And means I can afford that monthly pedicure …

Do I run business planning and forecasting?

Yes. My assistant and I sit down each month to review commissions and income to see exactly what's happening.

I also check in with my bookkeeper each week to work through the expenses. Annually, my bookkeeper and accountant and I meet to go over what's happening in my various businesses and trusts, and catch up prior to the end of each financial year. My accountant is also at the end of the phone for me whenever I have a new bright idea or want to start a new company or business idea. She's a great sounding board and can point out issues I may not have thought of.

Do I have a favourite form of investment?

I believe in a diversified portfolio for cash or monetary investments. I also like to invest small amounts in alternate assets like art and wine or digital currency. My husband and I also invest in properties because he's very handy and can add value to whatever we build or buy.

Aside from that, investing in personal growth is a total favourite of mine. I've done leadership courses, philanthropy visits to Africa and annually participate in conferences to learn more about business and to offer better services to my clients. This, in turn, improves the value of my business over the long term.

Ongoing learning is also a favourite and I read every day. I can't sleep at night if I don't invest some time in reading. It doesn't matter if it's a novel, regency romance, self-help or leadership book, something written by a friend or keeping up with what's going on in the *Outlander* series, I have to read! Seriously, I'd read toilet paper if it had printing on it …

> We all admire the wisdom of people who come to us for advice.
>
> Arthur Helps

Business gurus

I've included people in this book who've taken that leap of faith and started their own businesses for good reason. They're incredibly inspirational for starters!

Many years ago, my assistant and I attended a Business Mastery course run by a local college. It was a refresher for me on all the things to include and consider when running a business, but also offered some new ideas to introduce our teams to as they supported us on our journeys. The course covered everything from cash flow management to marketing. Not long into the first day, my assistant commented to me, 'It's fairly easy to work out who the business owners are, and who the employees are.' I asked, 'How's that?' She replied, 'You just think differently.'

I guess I'd never thought about that before. I suppose it really does take a special something to be able to walk away from the safety and security of a regular wage, back yourself and unleash a new or revamped business on your local community, or even the world. It doesn't always work and even the idea can be incredibly daunting. Plenty of well-meaning friends and family tell us we're completely nuts and sometimes, okay regularly, we even wonder if we are. We put up with sleepless nights, going without and more hours than we ever thought we'd need to invest ... but for a lot of people that spark burning inside just can't be ignored. That belief in the product or service we know we have and the knowledge we can make a difference.

Knowing that you're responsible not just for the wellbeing of yourself and your own family but for those who come to rely on you for their weekly wage is huge. Good times and bad follow each other, and it's pretty easy to lose your mojo and want to throw it all in – before you think back to why you started, and move on with a new lease of life. And then the cycle happens all over again. And, of course, as our businesses grow, they would be impossible to maintain without the hard work and loyalty of the teams who support us.

Most of the gurus featured here weren't savvy entrepreneurs with business know-how when they started out. Instead, they learnt along the way and then educated themselves later. They're men and women from all walks of life and from country and city upbringings. Some are parents, others not; they are partnered or single, and some are remarried. Most are from working-class families who came to their careers from interesting paths. Some followed the traditional high school to university to employee to business owner path; others were early entrepreneurs, straight out of (or even during) school. I wanted to know how they got to where they are and what lessons they have for us, and so asked a similar series of questions to all the gurus.

In this part are the stories from those who've carved out their entrepreneurial journey and trod their own paths. I hope the included lessons learned from families and their own treatment of money, along with the ideas they'd like to pass on, teach or even inspire you.

Emma Isaacs

Founder and global CEO Business Chicks

'I believe that it doesn't matter how much you earn; it's what you do with it that counts.'

@emmaisaacs
@businesschicks

Emma Isaacs is the founder of Business Chicks, a now global support network for women in business. Today, Business Chicks produces over 110 events annually, publishes a quarterly magazine called Latte and facilitates thousands of new connections every week for its members and over 250,000 social media followers through its engaging content. In 2016, Emma packed up her young family (she's mum to five kids) to move to California, where she launched the US arm of Business Chicks. She now has three US cities under her belt and global domination is on the radar.

Emma can take something good and turn it into something spectacular. After seven years of running her own recruitment business, which she acquired at just 18, Emma was invited to a small event run by a group called Business Chicks. After hearing the business was for sale, Emma took a leap of faith and bought it.

In many ways, you could say that Emma is unconventional in the way she does business – she treats her team like her family, she knows the Business Chicks members by name and she signs off emails with kisses – but that's what makes Emma and the business so unique and, I have to say, I'm up there as one of her number one fans.

Emma has spent time with some of the world's greatest thought leaders including Sir Richard Branson, Bill Gates, Sir Bob Geldof and Arianna Huffington. She is a highly sought after keynote speaker and media commentator on topics around female leadership and entrepreneurialism and has been featured in BRW, Cosmopolitan, The Sydney Morning Herald and The Age, The Australian Financial Review, InStyle and Marie Claire, and on Sunrise, Sky Business News and The Today Show.

Emma is the past president of the Entrepreneurs Organisation and actively mentors a number of female entrepreneurs and business owners.

I met Emma when I was still new in business and had decided to strike out on my own. I was looking to join a networking group that would support me as a woman in business, and had tried a lot of local and national groups that, while well established, just didn't seem to fit my own personal groove. All had too many versions of 'Business Card Bob' handing out cards and pushing their agenda without any real form of connection. I loved to introduce and connect people, but didn't find that people were always comfortable referring financial advisers, especially if they hadn't used my services, which is completely understandable.

After some Google style soul-searching, Business Chicks came onto my radar and I decided to give them a try. The first event I attended played host in Brisbane, Queensland, to the amazing Dr Catherine Hamlin of the Hamlin Fistula Hospital in Ethiopia, whose tireless years of continuing work training midwives completely blew my mind. And I can't even begin to describe the 'Business Chicks Vibe'. You truly have to be there at the events with hundreds of like-minded women to appreciate the buzz!

Since then, at Business Chicks events I've seen Sir Bob Geldof, Sir Richard Branson, Ariana Huffington, Magda Szubanski, Seth Godin, Nicole Kidman and so many more. I've travelled to every state of Australia that Business Chicks presents in, visiting clients and attending events. I knew very early on that I'd found my tribe. The following questions help you understand that 'Business Chicks Vibe' a little more. For more from Emma, check out @emmaisaacs and @businesschicks.

I was the eldest of three children, and had an idyllic childhood. I come from a lower-middle-class family and we enjoyed a suburban lifestyle – we played cricket on the street and got lost in the neighbours' backyards for hours on end. Family holidays were a road trip down the south coast of New South Wales or, if we were lucky, to the Gold Coast in Queensland!

We never wanted for anything and lived in a beautiful home that Dad built. Mum worked in the home until we were all out of school and really gave us the best start in life. I could read and write anything before I went to school thanks to Mum, and that really started me off with a confidence for learning and a curiosity to explore as much as I could. In kindergarten, the teacher would set me up with a book in front of the class, and go and make herself a cup of tea while she got me to read to the class.

Growing up, I sort of felt there was a bigger world out there for me to explore, and I knew from a very early age that I wanted to not just be financially independent, but financially successful too.

Our next-door neighbour owned the restaurant up the road, and I'd always beg her for a job. She'd continually tell me that I wasn't old enough yet and I'd promise her that I wouldn't let anyone know my age. She eventually relented and I started working just before it was legally permitted. I was completely committed and hard-working and tried to go above and beyond for every customer I'd meet. I'd make sure I was on time for every shift and be as friendly and upbeat as I could. While my friends were out partying in their teenage years, I was working, working, working. And I loved it!

Where did you learn about money?

I've had a couple of big influences in my life when it comes to money and wealth creation, but the one who first comes to mind is my grandfather. Poppy was always exceptionally frugal with his wages as a boat builder. He never earned much, but that never stopped him from being incredibly astute with his money. His first big investment was his house (which, at 84, he still lives in to this day) and he worked hard to pay off that mortgage. His investment choice was stocks and he bought all the big blue-chips when they were under a dollar each. He would re-invest the dividend every time and, over the years and decades, those shares increased in value dramatically. He isn't a speculative investor. He preferred the big corporates and would read and research voraciously. He was also never showy with his money – he always drove very modest cars and never spoiled us. It was only later in life that he started to share his wealth with his daughter (my mum) and help us all out from time to time. The biggest lesson he taught me was that you don't need to earn loads to start investing, and everyone can start some-where. While I've chosen business and property as my main wealth creation vehicles, what I've taken from him is a mindset that anything's possible with a little hard work and small efforts over time.

Have you had any financial setbacks? If so, how did you recover?

I've had plenty of financial setbacks and, in a lot of ways, feel most financially challenged in my current situation. I moved our family (husband and at the time four young children under seven) to Los Angeles last year and have spent a considerable amount getting Business Chicks off the ground here. California has exceptionally high tax rates – so, for example, the property we bought comes with a $36,000 land tax bill each year. These are the sorts of things you just don't know when you emigrate to a new country.

Health insurance is exorbitant and the cost of living is a lot higher too. There are, of course, exceptions to that rule – childcare is more affordable and so are cars! The challenge is building a strong credit score here in the US, which is a total minefield to navigate. It doesn't matter what wealth or asset base you have built in your home country, it's like starting from scratch all over again. So, after a year here, I still don't have a credit card (ludicrous!) and run everything through debit cards. We had to buy our car outright and our mortgage when we first arrived here was at a whopping 9 per cent interest rate as well. All these factors combined led to quite a bit of financial stress that we're only just starting to come out of now.

The other financial setback we've endured as our family has grown (we now have our fifth child) is the sheer cost of ensuring all their needs (and ours!) are met. I never really subscribed to the whole fear mongering about how much it costs to have a child – turns out I was completely ignorant, of course. Every time we head back to Australia, that's seven airline tickets to buy (and we always try bring a nanny too, so makes that eight tickets!) and if we're doing that trip two or three times a year, you can see how it adds up.

Working full-time in a growing global business means I have a couple of nannies and people around to help out with the running of the house and our kids, and these costs (not to mention the education and school fees) all add up. I'm confident, though, it'll all be worth it (or we'll go broke trying). It's times like these I'm grateful I built a strong financial base from a very early age – my investments and financial 'nous' means I can afford these luxuries and the lifestyle we lead.

What's the best financial advice you've ever been given, and who was it from?

Start early and just start somewhere. I can't tell you who taught me that – perhaps I read it somewhere – but the idea has always struck me as a really important one. When you're young, it's difficult to have foresight about the future – you just want to live to your fullest and hope that everything will be okay.

It doesn't matter how much you earn or how little you have - it's about building a discipline and building your confidence around money and investing. There are many micro-investing apps and products you can look into such as Acorns, which is well worth exploring. And believe you can! Wealth creation is about mind-set more than anything else.

As a legacy for your children, what would you like them to learn about money?

I'd like my children to not have any fear around money, and for them to understand that money is just an energy - it comes and goes and is mainly attributed to your mindset. I'd also obviously love them to have a generosity around what money they have and would love to see them using their wealth to help others.

Do you have a personal or family budget? Do you stick to it? Does it guide your spending?

My husband and I sit down fortnightly to talk about our finances. It's not always a comfortable chat, but it's necessary. We talk about what's coming up, what we're investing in, where the potential roadblocks might be and how we can better our situation. It's a discipline that a coach helped us develop together, and it's been fantastic for our relationship and for the family's wellbeing. Too often people just ignore their financial situation, hoping it will improve or that the problems will go away - there's a lot of ugly stigma surrounding money - so we just want to try and be as open and honest as we can with each other about what's going on.

You have a business - how important is annual forecasting and budgeting?

Financial acumen is so important in business - it can make or break you. Knowing your financial position and not sticking your head in the sand is paramount to any businesses success. I invest heavily in having the right people (inside and outside of my business) who can spend time in the numbers and report back on our results and any areas of concern. Having the knowledge and the confidence to make strong decisions based on your financial position is crucial in running a successful business.

Do you use or have you ever used a financial adviser? Do you see a benefit in dealing with a professional?

Yes, I have. There's a huge amount of benefit to be gained from seeking professional advice. Advisers can help bring clarity and expertise to your wealth creation goals and help you see a path to whatever you're trying to achieve. I try to have regular check-ins with my advisers and they help keep me on track.

What's your favourite form of investment?

For me, it will always be my business interests, but property comes a very close second. I've also invested in a number of other businesses outside of my own, so enjoy angel investing, where I'm able to assist with capital for business start-ups that I believe in.

My key take-outs

I love Emma's tip to just get started. We procrastinate over so many things and, before we know it, months or years have gone by before we actually start. Starting small and building a regular savings habit is vital. Even if you have no nest egg to start with and can only manage $25 per week, after two years, you'll still have $2,600 that you never had before. And you then might be able to add tax returns or money gifts to this and pop it into a high yield cash account to watch it grow.

I also believe that it doesn't matter how much you earn, and that it's what you do with it that counts. I know many people on seriously enviable incomes who live a lavish lifestyle and have no assets to show for their years of work. Whereas others I know, who are on much more modest incomes, have gone without and slowly built a nice little portfolio or nest egg for themselves. Where will you start?

I also love that Emma was so willing to 'have a go' and back herself from a very early age. Often, we can talk ourselves out of something before we've ever given it a red hot crack. Taking a small networking group and turning it into the global business it is today has been an incredible journey, and Em has learned along the way. She certainly didn't start out knowing exactly how to take her group international, yet that's exactly what's happened over time.

I also like that she wants her children to have no fear around money, and that will only come through knowledge. Hopefully, this book is a part of you peeling back the layers or mystery around money on your own journey and will lessen any fears you have. Do you believe that you even have fears about money? Never having enough? Not knowing what to do with too much?

Giving back is also a great lesson. Often, we don't stop to think how truly 'lucky' we are and privileged to live in a developed country. Sure, it comes with a whole other set of problems, yet most of us have no issues with food, communication, shelter and clothing. Helping those who have less is extremely rewarding.

> If it is going to be, it's up to me.
>
> Brian Tracy

Alison Hill

Psychologist, head mechanic
and CEO Pragmatic Thinking

'We now keep a close eye on the
figures, work out where to invest
in the business and make sure
our "business and life" strategy
meets our family's needs.'

@alihilltweet

27

Ali Hill is a registered psychologist and CEO at Pragmatic Thinking, a motivation and behaviour strategy company. She is co-author of the top business book Dealing with the Tough Stuff: How to achieve results from key conversations, *and author of* Stand Out: A real world guide to get clear, find purpose and become the boss of busy. *Off the launch of Ali's new book, she has released a professionally recorded Podcast series called* Stand Out Life - *conversations with influential women (and a few men) about what it takes, the mess and success, to live boldly in a busy world.*

Ali is a regular on Channel 9 and has regular articles published with the Fairfax Group (including in The Australian Financial Review, The Sydney Morning Herald *and* The Age), News Limited *(The Daily Telegraph *and* Courier Mail), and* The Huffington Post.

Her work has also found its way inside a few big businesses you might have heard of - such as PepsiCo, Siemens, McDonald's, Sydney Trains, BHP Billiton, Bond University, Griffith University and BlueCare, just to name a few. Ali presents her unique and authentic message as a sought after international keynote speaker and MC, where she engages her audience with humour, practicality and real-world thinking.

I first met the lovely Ali through our mutual love of Business Chicks. We'd found ourselves at a few of the same events around Australia and realised we share the same home town of Queensland's Gold Coast.

Ali was kind enough to support my fundraising efforts when I chose to partner with The Hunger Project and visit Uganda, having to raise a minimum of AU$10,000. Ali had already been on a similar adventure herself to Malawi, so had been down the fundraising path for her trip. She spoke at one of my fundraising events and I've also been privileged to hear Ali speak at various other business leadership and charitable events.

Ali was raised in country Australia, the middle child sandwiched between two brothers to parents who were lifetime public servants. Because Dad worked in forestry, they were always living in beautiful leafy areas. Mum took 12 years off to raise her brood before returning to work as a teacher and completing her master in education.

Ali's mum and dad definitely believed in leaving school, studying, working hard, being loyal and living within their means. Family holidays were saved for and a three-week overseas trip to Tonga was even on the cards when Ali was eight. Ali doesn't remember a lack of money, but there was certainly no splurging or big impulse spends. Both her parents would come to rely on generous government superannuation packages after retirement, and a few personal investments in blue chip shares.

Her money lessons from childhood were about hard work and finding a good job – and education was a must. She even gave babysitting and cleaning a try in her teens and some of the money saved from this went towards a gap year she took after high school, teaching in the UK in Cornwall and backpacking through Europe.

It wasn't until Ali met her partner (now husband), Darren, and they went into business for themselves that taking money seriously even came up on her radar. Together, they'd moved to Darwin, had the first of two children and launched their behaviour and motivation strategy consulting business. While Darren was doing an undergraduate degree and working, Ali was home with the baby doing an honours degree, and so living frugally became important. A basic budget ensured that they covered their bills and could feed themselves, with not a lot left over for extras.

Running the business from home meant low overheads and a good profit margin and things, thankfully, grew quickly.

The plan when starting the business was that they had to replace their earned incomes within a 12-month period, or it would all be over and they'd go back to their jobs. Thankfully, this goal was achieved in six months – and then doubled again in the next six months – through consulting and training.

A potential setback raised its head when one customer was unsatisfied with the work that some of their trainers were providing and they thought they'd have to refund a large consulting fee very early in the piece. Thankfully, the client was happy with the value that Darren and Ali provided themselves, and they learned a great lesson about how their profit was derived through value.

So, now you know a bit more about Ali and her story, the following provides a bit more detail (and you can follow Ali via @alihilltweet).

Have you ever had any financial setbacks?

When we packed up our business in Darwin, sold it and moved to the Gold Coast, we opened a new office, came up with a new name, hired an employee and thought we'd arrived – and that the work would just roll on in. Needless to say, it didn't. We were not savvy at all about money, but I think until that stage, we'd been successful 'despite ourselves'.

We weren't watching the dollars and cents. We had no accountant and are still repaying some directors' loans we'd taken from those days. Looking back, we were very naïve really.

So how have you recovered?

We found ourselves a great accountant to work with. It took about four tries to find someone who not only was like-minded and in a similar place to ourselves, but also could deliver the value and advice we needed.

He provided us with some amazing lightbulb moments and even offered a few 'smackdowns' to get us in the right head space. Once we got excited when he suggested an investment option to us that could return over 20 per cent. When he then said it was by investing in our own business, it really made sense.

We now keep a close eye on the figures, work out where to invest in the business and make sure our 'business and life' strategy meets our family's needs. Often, we'll come up with what we think is a great idea and he'll ask us 'Yes, but is it smart?' He definitely provides the focus we need.

What lies ahead?

We've just employed our 16th staff member and have been investing heavily in having a business that isn't dependent on me and Darren being there to run. We learnt that lesson the hard way – when we took a month off, the figures dipped badly for the quarter. It was a bit of a wake-up call when the accountant pointed out to us how so intrinsically important to the income we were, and we needed to work on that so we truly had a 'business'.

This year we plan to have a family holiday in France for one month so that will really be the litmus test to see how well the business now runs without us.

How do you think our beliefs affect us when it comes to money?

Nearly all of us hold limiting beliefs around money. We don't want to seem greedy and think it's wrong, or even bad, to earn what we think is too much. We feel that we shouldn't ask for more than we need and this definitely holds us back.

If you want to get past these beliefs, it's important to invest in your own personal development, which pays huge dividends, or seek professional help to coach you through identifying your own personal beliefs that could be impacting on you, and then work through them.

Do you stick to a budget?

No, we don't have a family or personal budget that we run. For the business, yes, absolutely. We know our break-even analysis and that this regularly changes. We know when funds are likely to come in, and that cash flow analysis and projection is a hugely important area for us to watch.

Thankfully, we've never needed to borrow to invest in or grow the business but maybe that's something we could look at in the future. Debt isn't something I'm really comfortable with, so I'd need to explore that.

What's your favourite investment?

Definitely our business and growing that. We do have our own home and have just invested in a holiday home for friends and family to enjoy in our favourite holiday spot, but property has never really been our focus. We like the liquidity of shares as a preference to property.

What ideas around money would you like to impart to your kids?

I'd love them to learn the benefits of compound interest and putting away into savings and retirement plans early.

And I'm sure I'll never really retire. I've been involved with The Hunger Project and their work in Africa, as well as Hands Across the Water (HATW), which supports children in Thailand. I'd love to someday run a foundation and even sit on a charity board. I'd love to leave the kids a legacy that giving back is really important and even a way of life.

My key take-outs

I love Ali's point that she and her husband were successful despite themselves. It's a great position to find yourself in! But it's where you go from there that really counts. I also enjoyed their realisation that their profit was derived from the value they provide. Often we think our product or service is where it's all at, and to an extent that's true, but people will often also pay for the value they perceive they're gaining.

And, of course, I love that partnering with a financial professional made such a difference to their outcomes. As Ali noted, it's important to find someone who aligns with your values and believes in what you're trying to achieve. Most professionals are good at what they do, but if their approach doesn't fit with what you're trying to achieve, you need to find someone who's a better fit.

Also, the plain and simple benefits of compound interest are fabulous to remember. Reinvesting interest to gain more interest is such a basic concept but often forgotten as we make things more complicated than they need to be.

Giving back is also a theme with Ali and finding something that we're passionate enough about to want to support can also be a rewarding journey. They say charity begins at home, but then, what comes next? Is it children's charities you'd like to support? Has your family been touched by a particular disease that you'd love to help eradicate? Has a local helicopter service saved a loved one? Is there someone in the community whose plight you'd like to help alleviate? Could just volunteering at a local school or shelter be enough? It's an interesting and fulfilling path to consider for those of us who've never thought about it before.

> You can choose courage, or you can choose comfort, but you can't choose both.
>
> Brené Brown

Babette Bensoussan

MindShifts

'We educated ourselves by attending various workshops and seminars to improve our own knowledge.'

@BabetteBen

For over 25 years, Babette Bensoussan has served as an adviser to organisations and business leaders around the world. A recognised global authority on competitive intelligence, and one of the most published business authors and well-regarded speakers in her field, Babette brings her own valuable insights to business leaders, entrepreneurs and seniors executives around the world.

In 1991, Babette founded the MindShifts Group, a leading consulting company based in Sydney, Australia, that specialises in business coaching, competitive intelligence and strategy. Babette has led the MindShifts Group through over 300 projects with Australian and Fortune 500 companies. Her skills and expertise have been successfully applied to a huge range of industries, and her clients have included (but are not limited to) aerospace, information technology, pharmaceutical, manufacturing, and financial services companies.

I first met Babette at a lovely BBQ lunch on a balmy Sydney day. I was fundraising at the time for my visit to Uganda with The Hunger Project and a supportive friend (who happened to be an amazing chef in a former life) decided to put on a couple of lunches, cater her heart out and invite groups of friends over to pay for lunch and share the feasting with all proceeds to the charity. What a gem!

Babette was one of the guests that weekend and, as it turned out, our paths had crossed previously, unbeknownst to me, when she'd been a judge of the Female Excellence in Advice Awards for the Association of Financial Advisers (AFA) that I'd previously entered.

As I found out personally when I engaged Babette for some coaching, she has as a strong passion for sharing her uniquely honed business experience with others. She is a qualified counsellor, coach and MBTI (Myers Briggs Training Indicator) practitioner, and is also at the time of writing the only executive coach certified in the Energy Leadership Index (ELI) in Australia – a unique and revolutionary leadership development tool used to determine engagement, performance and success abilities in work and life. The tool facilitates in assessing, harnessing and enhancing personal and professional leadership qualities.

So, with that impressive bio, I wanted to dig a bit deeper and find out a little more about Babette's family history.

As it turns out, her family are French Moroccan and migrated to Australia when she was just a toddler. Her father, a professor, was the family breadwinner and her mother a stay-at-home housewife with three children. This was a very traditional migrant family in 1950s Australia. Babette and her two younger brothers grew up between cultures, with a French–Jewish home life and typical Aussie school life.

Her parents believed implicitly in working hard to make a good living. Debt was something to be avoided at all costs and if you wanted anything, you needed to earn it. There were no such things as handouts. Money came solely from hard work. By 15, Babette was getting pocket money for doing household chores and had begun her first job as an usherette at a local cinema. She was also a pharmacy assistant and always worked during her school holidays.

Her parents gave their children no formal financial training but taught by example: save up, don't expect any windfalls or inheritance and don't take on too much risk. Making ends meet was always the first priority. After her father took some losses dabbling in the stock market, he became even more risk averse.

Babette's answers to my series of questions follow. You can also find out more about her through @BabetteBen.

Well, that would have to be the lessons I learned from the classic book *The Richest Man in Babylon* by George Clason. I loved the idea of setting aside some money for savings, some for giving back and some for spending. It just clicked with me and made sense. I've adopted that method and have different accounts for different needs through to this day.

I also had a close friend who was a financial adviser and she taught me all about different asset classes like cash or fixed interest or shares, and to be sure to diversify my investments by spreading them around. My husband loves property and would invest totally in that if he could, but I like to spread the risk. I'm really quite cautious and conservative by nature, probably as a result of my upbringing.

Do you have a budget that you stick to?

Not a formal personal budget, no. My husband and I get together once a year to work out how much our annual spend is likely to be and to see what we've spent over the past 12 months. It's a loose spending plan, but we're approaching semi-retirement and need to start making sure we're putting enough away now to cover future years where our incomes won't be as high.

For my business, yes. I understand that cash flow is key. Being a consultant, it's often 'feast or famine' for income, but I do know my break-even point and when expenses are due. I have studied corporate finance so understand the importance of this.

Have you ever used the services of a financial professional?

Yes, we have in the past, with mixed results. My first adviser was a friend and she spent a lot of time educating me on various investment options and the importance of not putting everything in a single type of asset. She was a fabulous asset and I value the educational work she did with me. We remain friends today.

After she retired, we tried two different financial advisers, without much luck. One seemed to be more interested in pushing product onto us and the other touted that they only charged set fees and it was all about the strategy rather than real results. Unfortunately, we lost with both. I just don't think they really took the time and effort to understand our background, conservative nature and preferences.

Since then, we've educated ourselves and attended various workshops and seminars to improve our knowledge. As a coach, I understand the importance of being coached, so we've learned and now manage our finances with our own self-managed superannuation fund, with assets that suit our profile.

What's your favourite form of investment?

My favourite form of investment is in personal education in self-development, always learning more. I've learnt about having an 'abundance mindset' and being coached. You'll never lose if you invest in yourself.

If you had one top financial tip to leave for others, what would it be?

Save more. I'd spend less on 'stuff' and buy better quality. I bought a fabulous suit in Italy once for $1,300 – for a jacket and two skirts. That probably sounds exorbitant, but 20 years later, that jacket is still fantastic. In the meantime, I've probably spent a fortune on cheaper suits that have only lasted a season or two before they've worn out. That's not true value.

I'm also all about being prepared. One of our goals in retirement is to travel a lot more, so we've been building·up our frequent flier points over the years to take advantage of all the miles when we can.

My key take-outs

I love Babette's reference to the book *The Richest Man in Babylon*. It's a great text for people starting out who want a good financial book to read, and its lessons are timeless. (For more tips on great books, see the 'Resources and further reading' section at the end of this book, where I've collated a list of recommended reading that you might like to try for yourself, both from people I've interviewed, along with a few of my favourites.)

Personal education is vitally important and how you choose to gain that is up to you. As Babette recommends, it's hard to go wrong when you invest in learning - whether through reading great books, listening to webinars or podcasts or attending seminars.

I also love her highlighting how important it is to find a financial adviser that's right for you. In part II, I spend more time on this, gathering together some tips and traps on what to look for when searching for an adviser or financial professional to suit you.

I also love Babette's tips on quality over quantity. My trips to Africa have certainly made me realise how much useless 'stuff' we end up with over time that we can totally live without! But one good quality piece of something we need can stand the test of time. This is where we truly learn the difference between what something 'costs' and its 'value'.

> You can't clean the room if you don't see the dirt. You can't change your thinking if you don't see the errors in your thoughts.
>
> Babette Bensoussan

Tina Tower

Entrepreneur and CEO
Nikhedonia Productions

'I believe money has an energy.
It's a vehicle and it ebbs and flows.'

@tina_tower

Tina Tower started her first business at the age of 20 and, by the time she hit 33, had built and sold three businesses, completed a degree, got married, had two children and started in the challenging world of building a national franchise network. Tina has run a toy store and tutoring centres, designed and licensed her programs, and franchised her business in 2011.

The idea for what would become Tina's franchise business began halfway through a primary teaching degree, when she saw a gap in the private education market and created her own tutoring centre. Finishing university two years later, she decided business was her first love and it was possible to touch children's lives on a more individual level through her schooling readiness and primary tutoring centre.

Tina developed a school readiness program from a solid foundation and a love of learning – and so her baby Begin Bright was born. To fit around her small children, Tina began licensing the Begin Bright program in 2009 and converted to a franchise system in 2011. During the five years of franchising, Tina built the Australia-wide network to 33 sites, before the company was acquired by international education company Cognition Education.

Tina has been featured in Sky Business, The Financial Review and was the 2014 Telstra Australian Young Businesswoman of the Year. Tina is currently the Entrepreneur in Residence for Business Chicks, Australia's largest female networking group, along with being a speaker, business coach and corporate trainer and launching Nikhedonia Productions, a film production company. The first two film projects are underway. You might be noticing a bit of a theme by now, but I also met lovely Tina through the Business Chicks network. She too was a premium member and had visited Uganda with The Hunger Project. I was planning and fundraising for my first trip when I met Tina at a Gold Coast Business Chicks event.

Since then, we've caught up at various events with the most memorable probably being a few days spent at the amazing Gwinganna Lifestyle Retreat in the Gold Coast hinterland. This was an amazing few days learning how to be present, recharge, detox and kick back with fabulous food, mostly grown on site, and maybe a swim or massage or two thrown in as well.

Tina is an eternal optimist and a huge advocate for living life out loud. She has two young boys and loves grabbing life by the throat and running with it. In a testament to living what you preach, Tina blends corporate capitalism with the hippy life, shunning the city to live on an acreage north of Byron Bay to get the best of both worlds. She encourages everyone to let their own light shine.

I also asked Tina a series of questions about what life was like for her growing up. I learned she is the youngest after five brothers. Her parents separated when she was just three and both found new partners. While being raised by her mother with three of her brothers, she came to understand a bit about small business because her parents ran a successful plumbing business.

Her parents believed in saving for a rainy day, being frugal and to hoard assets once they were acquired. Building a nest egg was a high priority and a 'buy and hold' strategy was their favourite.

Although this approach seems typical of those in the previous few generations, it eventually became a lesson in what Tina didn't want to do. As you've probably understood by now, Tina is all about 'having a crack.' She's prepared to go all in, and is happy to learn, especially from her mistakes. Some of her responses to my questions follow, and you can find Tina via @tina_tower.

Have you had any financial setbacks?

Yes, my first was very early. I'd read Robert Kiyosaki and Anthony Robbins during my teenage years and worked an extra job to be able to afford my first home at the age of 18. At that time in Australia, the federal government was extending the First Home Owner Grant' to those who hadn't purchased property before, as long as it was owner-occupied.

I purchased a property and took the grant, but I never lived in the property and rented it out for the income. Of course, I was found out and had to pay the grant money back and, within a very short space of time. I was begging and borrowing from everyone I knew. I learnt the hard way not to do 'dodgy' things.

I still believe that I have time, and I'm young enough to take calculated risks, go big, lose and go again. While I'm still in my thirties, that's fine, but that will probably change when I reach my mid-forties. No doubt I will want to reassess the risks I take in view of having a shorter investment time frame.

What's the best financial advice you've ever been given?

I've read and learned so much over the years. From my reading and research, I've developed my own philosophy, which is to invest in a way that means I can live to 150, but live as if I'll die tomorrow.

I'm a voracious learner and some of my favourite books are by Kim Kiyosaki, such as *It's Rising Time!* and *Rich Woman*. I've never been afraid to ask questions, even the ones we're often told it's rude to ask. I'm not doing it to be nosy about people's situations, but because I really want to learn, and I think people realise that and are happy to share, even if they're a little uncomfortable at first.

I loved learning 'not to put all your eggs in one basket' and when I learned about a risk profile and what other investment options are available, I really researched it. I wanted to know about shares and commodities and how they worked and include them in my portfolio too. I research everything!

What lessons would you like your children to learn about money?

I don't want them to ever trade time for money.

I believe money has an energy. It's a vehicle and it ebbs and flows. I learnt a lot in Uganda about how far money can go when it's needed, and want to help others and for my children to learn to want to make the world a better place.

I've found that the more generous I've been, the more money seems to flow. There's been times when we've had to tighten the belt and go without steak and salmon and life's luxuries, and settle for baked beans on toast, but that's okay too.

Do you have a personal or family budget?

Absolutely, yes. We look at this each year and set funds aside for what we'd like to do for holidays and gifts. I'm also aware of our outgoings and what we spend on insurances and utilities. I love having it all planned on Excel.

My husband and children are very supportive and have put all their bets on me and that's paid off. My husband is a completely different style of investor to me, very cautious and he makes me question everything. That's so valuable in our partnership. There's nothing better than being home with the kids and being able to plan our activities together.

We discuss whether it's best to have one big holiday each year or three or four smaller ones and collaborate on those sorts of decisions.

How important is annual forecasting and budgeting in your business?

Extremely; I still can't believe business owners don't do this!
I work closely with my accountant to monitor the figures at least

fortnightly because it's a living, breathing and changing piece. I'm aware of when all major outgoings are due and break-even points. It's too important to let it go.

What are some lessons you've learned in business?

I've learned to focus on the end game and be really okay to go without. I started franchising at 27 and it meant big sacrifices. Our family has lived in a small unit, slept on mattresses at my mum's and gone without holidays because of the long-term focus. I'm not all about instant gratification. All these moves, though, were calculated and strategic and about ensuring Begin Bright would be successful.

I've also learned that it's not how hard you work or how much you make; it's what you do with it. I've seen people on lower incomes be very successful with their money and others on huge incomes waste it all.

I've learned to ask questions. I have no filter when it comes to getting information and am happy to ask what many don't or won't. I'm genuinely interested in how people have made the most of what they have and what they've done to achieve their goals.

The trip to Uganda also taught me about perspective. My version of poor and their version of poor couldn't have been more different. I felt compelled after that to give back and make a difference. And, funnily enough, it's shaken up some personal beliefs. I now understand that the more I earn, the more I can contribute. That changed everything for me.

We're often taught that getting more equals greed, but I look at things differently now. Being immersed in a developing country was a pivotal moment and gives me a different focus for acquiring wealth.

For return on investment, I don't think you can ever go past your own business, which for many people is quite complex. If you want to keep it simple, invest in property. It's an easy, 'set and forget' strategy.

My key take-outs

I've already added Tina's book suggestions to the further reading list at the back of this book. There are some great ideas there.

It's also a great tip to do your research! You don't ever want to be in a position where you need to return money like Tina had to with her housing grant.

Also, her lesson for her children about not wanting them to trade time for money is a little different. Many are of the view that that's how life works and this is exactly what they want their children to learn really early. This contrarian belief is really entrepreneurial and probably why she's been so successful with her business ventures. What's your view?

I also love that Tina has had a total change of mindset around money or wealth and whether that equals greed or selfishness. She now believes that the more successful she is, the more she is in a position to be able to give back. That's a great gift and a really beautiful way to be able to look at and appreciate our successes.

Do what you have to do until you can do what you want to do.

Oprah

Tanya Targett

Entrepreneur and creator of
Winning Publicity Formula

'Money is everywhere and it's
available. I've learned about an
abundance mindset and I've been
able to see it in action for myself.'

@tanyatargett

Often referred to as the 'Media Darling', Tanya Targett is a former investigative news journalist who knows how to 'get the story'. In fact, she has won an award for Best News Story. A successful business woman in her own right, Tanya has used media and publicity to build two six-figure businesses in both the retail and service industries. Tanya is quoted and featured in national and international media – including on national TV – as an industry commentator, and is now also a media and publicity coach. Her inspirational teachings have seen her students also showcased in national and international media publications – including prime-time TV.

Described as a 'change maker', she gives small business owners and entrepreneurs permission to chase their passions and dreams while creating profitable, secure businesses. She is based on the Gold Coast in Queensland, Australia, but runs media and publicity training globally via her online personal brand. She is also an adventure-preneur who loves to kite surf and paddle board in her downtime.

I first met Tanya Targett when I wanted to learn a little more about getting involved in the media. I had no clue about how to do a media release or get more exposure, so researched on Facebook, came across Tanya and her business Headline Hunter and enrolled in one of her courses. Who said Facebook advertising doesn't pay off?

As we started our chat, Tanya told me she is the younger of two girls. She was born in the United Kingdom but spent between three and six in the Middle East before moving to Australia. She attended around 10 different primary schools and four different high schools, making her an expert on fitting in. During her schooling and as 'the girl who spoke funny', Tanya was a mark for bullies but feels that the ability to be able to move around and move on definitely gave her advantages too.

Tanya started making a name for herself quite young and was suspended from school for protesting over injustices – she took a story to a local news channel on the issue of asbestos at her school, for which she was dragged to the headmaster's office and given some time off school. As you can probably imagine, she eventually became an investigative journalist.

These days, and now that Tanya has her own daughter, she would like to think she's gone from rebel to role model. She has presented at more than 100 events, including corporate breakfasts and lunches, workshops, expos and industry-specific conferences, along with the international marketing summit LaunchCon in Los Angeles.

She has been a speaker for Jeff Walker's Product Launch Formula 'Launch Club' and LaunchCon, Women in Business Expo (at Bond University), Chamber of Commerce Queensland (for numerous chapters), Healthy NetWealthing (Sydney, Brisbane and the Gold Coast), Gold Coast Business Expo, Success Women's Network, Empowered Mums and Key Business Network. Her answers to my questions follow, and you can catch her via @tanyatargett.

What lessons did you learn from your parents about money?

The thought that stands out the most to me was that they believed that people who had money were bad, usually drug dealers. The message was loud and clear that you had to break the law to get ahead. I was told working hard would never be enough. I'd never be able to get ahead no matter whatever I did, unless I broke the law.

It's funny, even now, when driving around and I see a nice home, the first thought is always, *Must be drug money*. It's amazing how ingrained those thoughts become. I very consciously have to change those patterns.

Yes. When the deadly inland floods hit Toowoomba in 2011, I lost everything. All my business stock was destroyed and I had to walk away. Thankfully, I didn't go bankrupt but was able to take time, trade through and clear my payments owing, including tax debts and credit cards. I paid everyone back and delivered on existing orders.

My biggest battle, however, was moving on from a financially and emotionally abusive relationship. When I met the man who would become my husband, I had confidence, a great job in the media, property and cash in the bank. At the end of our relationship, everything had been signed over to trusts that he controlled. There was nothing left in my own name.

I was constantly told how bad I was at managing money. I was even told to 'stop playing around with the media' and to get work on a cash register at a local supermarket. It was basically an ultimatum. It was only when my daughter burst into tears and said, 'That's not who you are Mummy' that I felt like I'd failed her too and knew with absolute certainty that we had to leave. I had to stash some grocery vouchers at a friend's place, with money I'd been able to skim from the family budget that could tide us over for a few months, and stayed in a house my friend rented under her own name for us. I left financially at my lowest ebb and emotionally bankrupt. I had nothing left and had to rebuild from the ground up.

My health suffered severely for a very long time as fallout from this event, and sometimes setbacks can still occur. I had a stroke and a series of seizures from the stress, but slowly I've managed to rebuild and carve out a great life for myself and my daughter. I'd truly hit rock bottom, but am proof that you can also recover.

I've come to realise that life really is all about the journey. The destination keeps changing.

What is some of the best financial advice you've received?

It was definitely around business structures and on running a business, and to work with the end in mind. It's a principle I use in all aspects of life, from writing media releases to my coaching businesses.

From personal experience, I've been taught that covering your income for a period of time is vital. Always have some money aside for whatever need arises. My tip is to have, at the very least, three months' income covered and set aside in an account.

Also, I've learned about legacy – leaving something valuable behind for the world – and that doesn't have to be financial.

What's your personal top financial tip?

Well, it's to women everywhere and based on my former relationship experiences: always have a secret bank account. And I mean completely secret.

Never go into anything with your rose-coloured glasses on. Put even $20 per week onto a grocery card if you're able to, even if you don't need to. But, never, ever completely surrender your independence. And if someone wants you to, run like hell!

What lesson would you like to leave for your daughter?

That money is everywhere and it's available. I've learned about an abundance mindset and I've been able to see it in action for myself. I've managed to build a six-figure business within six months and have a six-figure income within 18 months of starting a business. I used every connection and resource I had available to me and know it works from first-hand experience.

I live by the motto now that the rules don't apply to me. We're often told by people, well-meaning or otherwise, that we're foolish or that what we dream 'can't be done'. Now I just shrug. I truly believe those rules don't apply to me. I've moved on from all the lessons in my childhood.

Do you run a personal budget?

Yes and no. I have accounts for different purposes – a grocery budget, savings, school fees, travel and adventure budgets. The ones that are most important to me (travel and adventure) get the most attention. I may not be quite as strict in some other areas. My philosophy is that I'll just make more money if I need to. I also use the app Moneysoft to manage my personal finances.

Does your business run a budget?

Yes, I think that's vital. I know what income is coming in, my return on investment, conversion, and which marketing gives me the best returns. I'm a bit slack with getting things done, but try to work closely with a bookkeeper and an accountant.

Have you ever worked with a financial professional?

In the past, yes. I wanted my retirement savings plan and insurances sorted and they were great at helping me out with that.

Do you have a favourite form of investment?

Yes, I quite like the share market for the long term.

My key take-outs

I found Tanya's story pretty amazing. The interesting lessons from her family from an early age right through to being financially abused were stories way outside what I'm personally familiar with. So many key lessons emerged from this interview on how to take charge of your life if you do find yourself in a financially abusive relationship.

Do the stories she was taught when young sound ridiculous to you? Or are they similar to what you've heard? If they sounded crazy, maybe you can check in with some of your own beliefs around money and question whether others may view them as a bit odd too? Is it time to let go of some of your limiting beliefs around money and look for new ways to view your financial story? That's a really empowering journey!

I love Tanya's resilience and ability to constantly bounce back, which is great for those who currently see no light at the end of the tunnel. Sometimes, our circumstances can seem overwhelming, but Tanya is proof that things can change and totally for the better!

Another great tip is to always have savings set aside to cover a few months' wages. It's a great lesson and will stand anyone in good stead when facing involuntary redundancy, prolonged illness, an accident or suddenly needing to cover a major expense that was totally unforeseen. Savings, along with a tailored income protection plan, can provide invaluable cover.

And for women currently in abusive relationships, I hope you can learn some great wisdom from Tanya to apply to your own situation.

> She believed she could, so she did.
>
> RS Grey

Michelle Hoskin

Standards International, UK

'The best strategy I've been taught for managing my own money has been to put my income into various pots.'

@littlemisswoww
@StandardsInt

Michelle Hoskin is well known for her endless enthusiasm and energy, infectious personality and unique outlook on what she describes as a 'magical industry' – financial services.

She has over 15 years' experience working with some of the leading and most successful financial services practices, and is internationally recognised as the font of knowledge and leading expert in identifying best practice standards of operation. She designs innovative solutions proven to eliminate the debilitating challenges faced by financial services professionals every day and helps advisory firms deliver a bit of WOWW! to their clients. Getting bogged down with legislation can help advisers lose their mojo and make it hard to deliver the WOWW! factor to their clients. Michelle helps them find that sparkle again and bring this back into their businesses and clients' lives.

As a member of the Professional Speaking Association, Michelle regularly presents to financial services professionals all over the globe, inspiring her audiences with the ideas and insights that she shares. I've added Michelle as a 'business guru' because she's not a qualified financial adviser, but her business does operate exclusively in the financial services sector.

I was lucky enough to hear Michelle speak when she toured Australia as a guest of the Million Dollar Round Table (MDRT) Association in 2016 (with her daughter, Ruby, in tow).

We were fortunate enough to connect again at the Annual Meeting of MDRT in Vancouver in 2016 where she was present-ing, and then again in Orlando in 2017 where she was catching up with clients, colleagues and coaches. And you might be pleased to know she's on a mission: to change the world, one financial adviser at a time.

In our chat, Michelle told me that she is an eldest daughter with a younger brother to a hard-working mum and dad. Her father worked very hard as a builder and in the coal mines, often doing double shifts and saving madly every year to spoil the family with a lovely two-week holiday to exotic locations like the Maldives, Ibiza and the Caribbean. Her mum was a young bride, having Michelle at 20, and worked mostly in the home raising the children, but fitting in some part-time work around this.

If Michelle learned one lesson growing up, it was that she was totally and utterly responsible for her own actions. She had to learn the meaning of proactive. If you want a new dress, get a job and save for it. If you want a paper run, ask and make it happen. If you want a baby-sitting job, make the phone call. If anything, this approach made her incredibly independent and a perfect candidate as a future entrepreneur.

Sheer drive was the main message she learned from her father's example of being an incredibly hard worker. If you want something, just get off your backside and get it! She can't imagine now what it must of cost for them to have those amazing experiences together as a family.

Having said that, she never remembers having a single conversation about money. No lessons were taught directly, either from within the family or through the education system, so she doesn't feel like she's ever really learned about money, not formally anyway.

Unspoken lessons, however, did filter through. Buying good quality over quantity was a family trait she inherited. Her bedroom held no cheap toys or touristy purchases. Just nice quality bed linen, one nice pair of jeans and good clothes – along with the memories of good quality experiences and holidays.

Another thing she learned was that there was such a thing as too much work and not enough life. A two-week holiday every year after slaving away for 50 weeks didn't seem right to her and she's now structured her own life to only work three days per week to spend more time with her daughter while she's still young.

Michelle's biggest financial setback came with the breakdown of her relationship. Not only did she separate from Ruby's father but also had to rebuild her finances and rehouse her ex-partner. She had to think very hard about different ways to make money to make ends meet. Putting the house on Airbnb for additional income was one of the 'out of the box' methods she used.

Her free time is super special to her and is spent 'making home' and enjoying quality fun time with her daughter, Ruby Mae.

So, again, I put to her some of the questions I've put to others. Her answers follow, and you can also find Michelle via @littlemisswoww.

What's the best financial advice you've ever been given?

Don't assume I know how to manage money. To this day, no-one has ever sat me down and said, 'Here's the deal with money.'

What I wish is that someone had sat me down early and said, 'Be commercial.'

I now utilise the services of Strategic Coach and have learned to value my time for what it is. Whenever I get a coaching client, I know I can add value and that's really important to me. Knowing my value has been great advice.

I like nice things, but I'm not very motivated by money.

The best strategy I've been taught for managing my own money has been to put my income into various pots. I allocate 20 per cent of my income to my daughter, 20 per cent to travel, 10 per cent for savings and 50 per cent for living expenses. If I need to raid one pot to top up another, I know that means another area in my life will suffer.

Do you have a top financial tip?

Yes: know your numbers. Innovate with how you earn money. Make the most of opportunities that present themselves and look for alternate income streams. That's being clever.

What would you like Ruby to learn about money?

I don't give her pocket money as a gift or salary every week.
I don't get paid for doing nothing. My world doesn't work like that, so neither does hers.

Money needs to be earned so she gets money for doing jobs. We also talk about her spending when she's saved enough. She can choose what she wants to buy, but she also needs to wear the consequences of her purchases. She can't go back and change things just because she changes her mind or hasn't really thought her decision through. We all need to understand our actions, like an impulse buy, can have consequences and this is one way of doing that.

I was once told that children spell LOVE, T-I-M-E and right now that's my priority – to spend as much time with my daughter as I can. So I've structured my business so that I'm only working three days per week at present.

Do you run a personal budget?

In my head, yes, I definitely track expenses. I know what bills are coming in and when. I buy what I want, within reason, and know what I can afford. If I want a treat, I need to feel that I deserve it and add more value somewhere. Even if I have the money to afford something, I want to save for it, to feel like I've worked for it. I have to work to earn it. It feels more valuable that way.

Do you run business forecasts?

Yes. It could always be better, but we run spreadsheets in the business and I have a full-time assistant who helps with that. I roughly know what the outgoings are in the business, and I regularly check that more is coming in than going out.

Yes, absolutely. I met with my adviser and said, 'This is what I'm worried about and this is what I'd like to happen in the future.' He filled in the gaps for me; it was perfect. I had no idea what I needed, but my adviser filled it in for me, and it was just what I needed.

The recent Manchester bombing and awful London fire in the apartment complex also made me rethink how fragile life is and I reassessed what I'd like to leave for Ruby, so I took out additional insurances to leave her better off if something happens to me. I know that she's very well taken care of, and that's important. I also took out more critical illness protection so if something happens, I have ample protection in place.

Good advisers are able to help us fill in the blanks in our lives. That's a great value add.

What's your favourite form of investment?

For me, it's definitely my business. We don't have compulsory pension savings in the UK and the government pension is not anywhere near enough to live off. We are introducing an auto-enrolment system but employees can opt-out of this.

My business is my main asset and I'll structure that for longevity. I'm training coaches to do what I do around the globe and will be looking to build passive income. I'll probably never fully retire, but structure the business to help fund my ongoing lifestyle or sell it to fund my retirement.

I'm also a part-owner in another business – the Ladder 87 company – and it's all about safety and community and teaching positive life skills. We have a 1987 firetruck called Dennis and we run options for children's entertainment, community events and specialist transport that's all about safety and wellbeing. I love being a part of that and will be in that for the long haul.

My key take-outs

I love that Michelle has a really balanced attitude towards time and money. Having a workaholic father has shown her that there's more to life and she'll never regret the extra time that she gets to spend with her daughter while she's still young.

I also like that her parents taught her very early that her financial future was up to her, and that seems to have pushed her down an entrepreneurial pathway.

It's interesting too that it's often only when disaster strikes that we reassess our own personal situations. My tip for this would be please don't leave it until then! Take the time to regularly assess your personal needs and circumstances and regularly review your financial needs. Set aside a regular time that's relevant for you. Maybe it's when you have annual leave or at the start or end of a financial year. Choose whatever works for you, but make sure you always arrange time to take stock and revise your current needs, budget, insurances and retirement plans.

Michelle's proactive training with Ruby earning funds and having to wear the cost of her actions is also a great start for her daughter's financial journey.

Of course, I also love her take on the value that financial planners can add. Financial planners and advisers being able to 'fill in the gaps' is a valuable resource you can tap into in life.

> I will not die an unlived life.
>
> Dawna Markova

Susanne Bransgrove

Founder, Families in Transition

'We spend a lot of time thinking about money and give it power that it doesn't need to have in our lives.'

@intransition01

Having spent much of her early career in and around the corporate banking and finance industry, both in Germany and Australia, Susanne Bransgrove experienced a variety of different approaches to business and leadership styles, and cultural differences. This exposure inspired Susanne to focus her attention and passion on family and business governance.

In 2014, Susanne founded Families in Transition, which focuses on supporting families in business with the most important journey they will ever face – generational transition.

I first met Susanne, lovingly known as Susu, when I was much newer at financial planning than I am now, and she was working as a business development manager for an investment company. She was assigned to me as a potential client to showcase her company's strategies and products and we became firm friends very quickly.

My business was still in its early stages, and I remember her asking me after a while if I thought it was worth it – that is, being self-employed and working crazy hours with a young family – while corporate life seemed to offer so much more. It was an interesting question, and certainly one that made me think, but once you've worked for yourself, you know you'll never get a better (or harder) boss!

I watched Susu move through her career, be made redundant and work through a few different firms in corporate finance before finally deciding to branch out on her own and start her own firm. Since then, both our businesses have grown, and she hasn't looked back on the decision to believe in herself and move on from building someone else's business.

Today, Susu helps multi-generational family businesses work through their family and business issues by supporting the individuals, the family and the business. Her passion, expertise and commitment to help these families in business manage their generational transition journey are unrivalled.

She is herself a third-generation family business owner (more on this in the interview), so she understands the complexities and challenges faced by families in business, and combined this experience and vision when she created Families in Transition to provide positive change. Families in Transition supports family businesses throughout the transition process by creating a journey that the family can easily follow and embrace.

Her passion and vision is to make a positive difference on a business front as well as a personal front, and to invigorate as many family and private businesses as possible by broadening her reach.

A self-appointed catalyst for change, her strength lies in her diverse experience and ability to lead groups, particularly families in business, through the change necessary to succeed. She is a compassionate leader with high expectations, and has the ability to build bridges between people and their perspectives, thus creating team cohesion and team power fuelled by a clear vision. While having compassion, she is outcome focused and it is natural for her to combine these skills.

I asked Susu similar questions to all my interviews, and her answers expand on these ideas. You can also find her via @intransition01.

I am the youngest of three, although I only ever lived with one of my siblings. I have two half-sisters because my parents had both been married before and each had a daughter from their previous marriage. I grew up with one sister, who is five years older than I am, and didn't spend much time with my other sister, who is eight years older, until I was around 18. We grew up in Bremen, Germany.

My parents were both born during the Second World War and, very naturally, scarcity was a major issue after the war finished.

It was hard to find a good husband in the '50s, as many of the young men had died in the war and not many children were born between 1938 and 1945. Many of the women were involved in rebuilding the cities, which had been destroyed in the war. They were referred to as *Trüemmerfrauen* or 'rubble women' and they held a critical role in getting the country back on its feet. It was a monumental task and my grandmother was involved, as were most other women of her age. My grandfather (on my mother's side) was a successful officer and a freemason and ran a packaging company. Both grandfathers were prisoners of war and amazingly came back alive and well but had to rebuild their lives.

For the women of my mother's generation, marrying a man who was from a wealthy family or had the potential to become successful was the best opportunity you could have. Secretarial school and marriage were the order of the day. Mum married her first husband to get out of home, but the marriage didn't work out. She later married my father, who was the heir to a successful business my grandfather very opportunistically bought after the war.

Typical for the times, my mother was a stay-at-home mum, responsible for looking after the kids, putting food on the table and entertaining guests when necessary, while my father helped build the family business. Our family business establishes accurate records of goods stowed on ships to inform the details included on the bill of lading. Dad is very good at what he does, but the introduction of containers changed everything and, although still profitable, it is a now much smaller business.

I grew up hearing conversations about business, and the issues my father faced with staff, unions and clients, and I believe that being part of these conversations has shaped my journey and my passion for what I do now.

Funnily, I always liked money, or the idea of it, and studied banking and finance in Bremen after school. Even my work experience in high school was in a bank.

My other passion was sport and hockey and I fell in love with Doug, an Australian hockey player who was living in Germany for a while. I came back to Australia with Doug for a year to check the lay of the land and we ended up getting married. We were together for around 10 years before going our separate ways.

What's the best financial advice you've ever been given?

My father encouraged me to spreadsheet expenses and helped me understand very early that annual payments need to be budgeted for on a monthly basis. It made sense for him to account for expenses and allow for future payments that need to be made rather than spend all the money.

I still remember the conversations he had with me when I bought my first car about splitting the annual registration and insurance bills over 12 months, and him showing me how to set a spreadsheet up to keep track and budget.

He still manages his finances this way.

It was good advice and I still have separate accounts for bills, spending and savings.

Yes, absolutely. I was in a relationship with a man who was fun-loving and perhaps a little irresponsible and with him I changed, actually abandoned, a lot of my formerly good financial habits. My partner was a very positive, big picture man with great ideas but when it came to being disciplined and doing the hard work to deliver, he tended to fall short. Of course, I couldn't see that at the time and I was very caught up in his personal self-belief and over-confidence that everything would just work out. I lost a lot of myself and ended up leaving the relationship with very little.

Coming from a very structured background, I had to become very good at dealing with chaos and had to rebuild from virtually nothing.

More importantly, I needed to rethink what success meant to me. From an early age, I thought that success was about a good job with a great salary, a title, a nice car, and good corporate bonuses. Money and the outward trappings of success had always been a very defining part of who I was.

When I left the relationship, I could only afford $100 rent per week and was lucky enough to be able to live with a friend until I was back on my feet.

I certainly didn't expect to get to 40 and, rather than having a big house, nice car, happy family and successful career, having to rebuild myself from the ground up, without all the trappings of what western society defines as success.

I am incredibly grateful that this experience has prompted a long – and on-going – journey of understanding who I am, what matters in life, what my values are and what I am passionate about.

Early lessons from my family included 'he who has money, controls'. More money means more control; less money is less control. Money has a very different meaning now and no longer takes pole position in my life. If you are in-line with your purpose and values and contributing to others in a positive way, the money will take care of itself. There is always a solution to shift things to be able to survive. If you have to ask for help, or learn to live without things you previously thought necessary, then that is okay too.

Money no longer rules the purpose of my working life. It is a by-product of what I do. We spend a lot of time thinking about money and give it power that it doesn't need to have in our lives.

A big lesson, and one that I still observe in other people, is that any decision based on greed or just financial outcomes is never a good decision. We need to balance wellbeing and satisfaction in our work decisions so much more than just financial implications. This is a complete turnaround in my thinking.

My father used money to control my mother and our family. He provided the budget for the family and it was set and we'd have to stick to it. He'd be happy to spend $20,000 on a Rolex, but would be unhappy with $5 spent on cheese. I'm only unlearning some of these ideas now.

Even my mother, in turn, was very influenced by status. It was all about what people were wearing, where they lived, what car they drove and who they associated with.

I don't have as much now as I once did, but I'm able to be more generous. I'm happy to support causes and have found that I don't miss the money that goes to support others. I was always afraid of giving something that I might later miss and that has changed totally for me. As it turns out, I don't miss what I give away at all.

Do you have a personal budget?

Yes, I do. I have a savings account, a monthly account and a spending account. I pay all my big bills like rent, electricity and so on up front each month.

I immediately put money into the savings account for holidays or big items and try to leave money there untouched.

How important is annual forecasting and budgeting in your business?

My business doesn't have a lot of overheads so I don't need to run too much of a budget or serious cash flow tools.

I do travel a little but clients mostly reimburse me for this. I'm always on top of what's coming in, though, and how much is in the pipeline moving forward.

What are some lessons you've learned in business?

If you want to start your own business, you need to be realistic about how long it will take to get the business cash flow positive. You will need to have a year's worth of fixed expenses covered, like income per individual employee plus start-up costs for stock or manufacturing or parts.

It does take longer than you think, so make sure you have enough capital, good supporters to lean on around you and don't give up on your dreams if it takes that little bit longer.

In established family businesses, an important lesson is to spend time and invest in preparing your next generation to be the best leaders possible, regardless of whether they are going to end up working in your business or not. Nurturing the next generation is incredibly important!

What's your favourite form of investment?

Cash is my favourite at the moment. I like being flexible and able to take advantage of opportunities. I'm still rebuilding from difficult times, which is likely why I like to be close to what I have available.

There will come a time when I'm comfortable enough to move away from cash but I don't want my fear to stop me from moving towards future or possibly more 'riskier' investments.

I love the dialogue and accountability available when working with a financial professional. Having somebody who can help you put a plan and strategy together that is right, and then hold you to working towards what you committed to is invaluable.

It puzzles me why people think they can put aside their emotional bias when making investment decisions or be disciplined with researching the various options.

I believe that financial professionals are invaluable to stop us from making uninformed decisions, based on emotions.

My personal financial adviser [yours truly!] has my absolute trust and I believe that her objective perspective, education and time and effort spent researching the various options will yield much better outcomes than I could ever deliver for myself.

For my business, I work with a bookkeeper, financial adviser and an accountant to help keep me on track, and I use them as a sounding board for business and financial decisions that need to be made.

My key take-outs

The personal journey that Susanne has been on over the past few years is quite profound. I had never grown up thinking that the universe turned on money, and it's been fascinating to watch her transformation away from this mindset and being a lover of corporate life to a more laid-back and loving approach. She seems calmer now that she's moved away from the power she once allowed money to exert on her. Although still rebuilding after the end of her relationship, she is also being a lot kinder to herself. This is a lesson we often need reminding of because we're often our own harshest critics and judges.

Based on her upbringing and the lessons she learned about money being about control, it been great to also see her embrace philanthropy and the understanding that giving doesn't need to hurt. She can assist others without missing the funds and feel good about helping. I also remember her devoting time and energy to assist others in the massive clean-up after the devastating Brisbane floods in 2011.

Stepping aside from the banking and finance corporate roles that were once her life has been very personally rewarding and I love Susanne's new thought pattern that if we're adding value, the money will take care of itself and is just a by-product of what we do. People are happy to pay for the value they perceive that we deliver.

> You were not created to live small and safe.
> You were created to live fierce and brave.
>
> Lisa Bevere

Business gurus summary

The stories in this part were pretty amazing. I loved that these people were the daredevils - the crazy ones who had that initial thought and the gumption to make things happen.

They were the ones who started something small and now run a business. They've not only taken charge of their personal financial future and that of their family, but also taken responsibility for the futures of their employees and their families too. It's a task I know none of them takes lightly.

Many understood the value of partnering with a financial professional and using them as a coach or a sounding board. Can you find someone who'll fill that role for you?

I also love that many of them have had to overcome some limiting beliefs or childhood lessons around money or greed, and that moving on from these ideas has been freeing. It's also allowed the opportunity for many to give back in ways they'd never previously thought possible.

It's always worth asking the question, 'What's holding me back?' and not just for financial matters. We often make excuses to not take that role, not do that bold thing we'd always wanted, not step up when offered something that scares us. It's easy to stay comfortable. But it's also a dead zone. No growth happens when we aren't constantly challenging ourselves.

Entrepreneurs truly have different thought patterns when it comes to making ends meet and thinking outside the square. Money is a tool and not something to be trading time for. Does this idea resonate with you or frighten you?

I found it also interesting that more had comprehensive business plans and cash flow forecasts in place rather than personal budgets, placing a much higher priority on their business inflows and expenses rather than putting food on the table or managing personal finances from a micro-management perspective.

I'd love to hear what other lessons you got from hearing the stories of those in business. Did something from one of the interviewees make a lightbulb go off for you?

> Here's to the crazy ones. The misfits. The rebels. The troublemakers. The round pegs in the square holes. The ones who see things differently. They're not fond of rules … You can quote them, disagree with them, glorify or vilify them. About the only thing you can't do is ignore them. Because they change things. They push the human race forward. While some may see them as the crazy ones, we see genius. Because the people who are crazy enough to think that they can change the world, are the ones who do.
>
> Steve Jobs (as part of Apple's 'Think Different' ad campaign)

Part II

Financial geniuses

Okay, most of the people included here probably do *not* think of themselves as financial geniuses. In fact, most of them may even cringe a little when they see that I've called them that! Not a single one of them became a financial adviser because of a burning childhood desire to do so. None of them left school ready to sign up for the next diploma intake or were knocking down the doors of the local planning offices to start an internship.

They range in age from their thirties to fifties; most have partners; some have children from former partners and/or current partners or are about to be parents; others don't. They're the sort of people you'll meet on the school run or see at the supermarket or helping out in their local communities. You know – just everyday people. We have yoga instructors to professional drummers in the mix here, and I'm sure you'll find their insights incredibly valuable.

I only include this as an introduction because a misconception seems to exist that most financial advisers have sharp teeth, a tail and horns, and know many mysterious and unimaginable ways to deprive you of your hard-earned cash. I wanted to set the record straight, up front. Consider yourself warned – they may not even look like what you think financial advisers should look like, whatever that is!

All the people included in this part are really small businesspeople who've studied up and increased their technical skills around money, and have a great desire to assist other people to do the same. They run successful planning practices around the world and their aim is to assist their clients to protect what they've already worked so hard for, and to help them grow wealth for their futures selves, their families and their retirement phases. They comply with rigorous licensing regimes, pay out large sums of money to be registered as advisers, ensure their professional indemnity premiums are covered and constantly grow their knowledge, keeping up to date with the never-ending changes to government legislation and their clients' constantly moving circumstances.

Because they are all highly skilled on the subject of money, in the interviews that follow I asked how they arrived at being an adviser and for some insights they've learned on the way about money. I wanted the top tips they share with their clients and the information they want their children to know about the subject of money.

For many, money is still a taboo subject. Some still include it on the banned dinner conversation list – along with religion, politics and sex. You know, all the interesting topics, really!

This is truly your chance to sit back, grab a coffee, a wine or your tipple of choice and take advantage of some of the amazing brains in the finance field, perhaps without ever having to sit in front of a planner. But then, after you get to know a few, maybe you won't mind so much meeting one in the flesh! (Please stop walking away from us at barbeques! We do have feelings too!)

Lea Schodel

Founder of Wellthy and
The Mindful Wealth Movement

'I always ask myself now if my future self will thank me for the purchase I'm buying with her income.'

@leaschodel
@wellthy

Lea Schodel is a qualified financial adviser and the founder of The Mindful Wealth Movement, a uniquely feminine program that empowers women to take control of their relationship with money and create financial wellbeing for themselves and their families.

As a financial planner, yoga teacher and writer, Lea is passionate about financial wellbeing and teaching women about money in a holistic and creative way. She runs online coaching programs, as well as wealth wellness events and retreats, which incorporate personal finance with mindfulness, yogic philosophy and life skills.

Lovely Lea lives on the Sunshine Coast (north of Brisbane) in my home state of Queensland. She's been in the financial advice industry since she was 19 and has a very different approach to providing client advice than many traditional advisers. Lea's approach centres on mindfulness and getting to know her clients' 'money personality'.

Lea and I both serve on the Queensland committee of the Association of Financial Advisers community Inspire, dedicated to raising the profile of women in financial services and improving financial literacy for our clients. We were both privileged to be finalists in the 2016 Female Excellence in Advice Awards, where I learned a little more about Lea's unique take on financial planning. Lea then took out the award, winning top spot in 2017 and becoming an amazing ambassador for women in financial services.

Lea happens to be the only girl in a set of triplets and has an older sister also. Her family moved between Australia and New Zealand a few times when she was younger and eventually settled in Australia to allow the children better education and tertiary options. Her siblings all took up the challenge. One brother has a PhD and works for Boeing, her other brother has an engineering degree and works for BHP and her sister has a degree in marketing and runs her own business. Lea decided uni wasn't for her but took up on-the-job training in the financial planner's business where she started and completed her diploma in financial planning before branching out into her own business (read 'black sheep' of the family!).

Lea's parents were serious renovators outside of their day jobs, flipping houses for extra income. Her dad was a sales manager and mum worked part-time. Raising a toddler plus triplets is no mean feat! That's four kids under four! Support from the government was incredibly limited back then and 10 hours per month assistance was all that was on offer. (I doubt that even covered the laundry time!)

Lea remembers that they'd always buy 'the worst house' and, as soon as it was renovated and gorgeous, it'd be time to sell and do it all over again. Perhaps that's part of the reason she moved to Japan to study for a year.

Lea went for two job interviews on her return to Australia from Japan. At that stage, she'd never heard of a financial planner, but she was offered both jobs and so had to choose between one in tourism that was over an hour's commute away and an admin role in a financial planning office closer to home. She jumped at the one closest to home. Lea soon settled into her role and served the function of what today would be known as a practice manager. Over time, Lea completed her diploma of financial planning and became a qualified financial adviser as well.

Later, Lea moved to the UK for a time for work. Full of naiveté and enthusiasm, she had no doubts she'd be hired based on her recently developed skills in her financial planning role, but found out the hard way that things don't always go as planned and ended up working in a bar. It was a rude awakening, but living off her savings was also a wake-up call and a great lesson. She had to manage her money to make ends meet. This was a lesson that plays an important role now in her own financial planning business.

The lessons Lea learned from her family around money were all about being careful. Money didn't grow on trees. A good education was paramount to getting a good job and earning well. Mum had the family budget firmly in hand and every cent she spent was recorded in a book she carried with her in her handbag, always.

In 2016, Lea was named Money Management's *Young Achiever of the Year* and was a finalist in the *AFA/TAL Female Excellence in Advice* and *ifa Innovator of the Year*. Lea's work has also been featured in many publications, including The Sydney Morning Herald, Entrepreneur Magazine *and* The Age, *and is a contributor to* Wanderlust, OM Times *and* Financy.

Along with managing Wellthy, Lea is treasurer and a director of Logan Women's Health & Wellbeing Centre, as well as co-founder of Yogic Journeys and lead wellbeing consultant for The Modern Careerist.

In the following questions, I wanted to find out more about Lea's unusual approach to planning. You can also find more from Lea via @leaschodel, @wellthy and @themindfulwealthmovement.

What can clients expect when they see you about their planning needs?

I'm very much focused on the *why* and the purpose behind the why. Someone might tell me that they want to save to buy a home or have an investment property. What I want to know is, *Why?* What are the emotions and feelings and purpose behind the purchase?

I use a program called 'Money Habitudes' with clients and we play a game that lasts for around 15 minutes. I do this with couples and individual clients to give me an idea of the clients' money personality. They'll fall into one of six categories, although we all have a bit of each characteristic in our personality. It's about what money means to us. Are we interested in security, planning, being spontaneous, giving, status or being careful?

My business is a social enterprise, built for profit and purpose, so everybody wins.

How do you deliver your advice?

I've moved away from the more traditional face-to-face and one-on-one meetings and want to impact more people, so have taken the one-to-many approach.

I run online courses where you can choose whether you want to go it alone or be guided through the course. We also grant a scholarship to a vulnerable woman, someone who's been possibly impacted by domestic violence or really wants to start getting a grip on how their finances work.

I also run community workshops to inspire (mostly women) around money. These offer practical advice, especially for those who've been victims of financial abuse.

We heavily use social media and have webinars, a member site and Facebook groups. We've also launched our first crowd funding campaign to be able to offer a large number of scholarships, which we're so excited has reached its tipping point.

Something that's a bit newer is the offer of retreats to our clients. I'm looking at running my first one in Bali this year in conjunction with Luna Jaffe from the United States.

Do you run a personal budget and, if so, what tools do you use?

Yes, I do. I utilise an app called MoneyBrilliant and I'm usually on it several times a day. I have different 'spending plans'. I'm very intentional and mindful about my own finances; that way I can maximise any opportunities that come my way.

It's also how I can 'practise what I preach'.

Do you follow a business budget?

Yes, my firm uses Xero and I'm always in touch with my accountant.

What's the best financial advice you've picked up along the way?

It probably sounds cliché, but I'm quite anti-credit cards. That, and 'don't spend more than you can earn'. I always ask myself now if my future self will thank me for the purchase I'm buying with her income. It keeps me from those impulse buys - knowing I won't be impressed with myself later for spending future Lea's money!

What main lesson do you like to impart to your clients?

Get very conscious of where your money is going. We have to be intentional - to tell it what to do, or wonder where it went!

What's your favourite form of investment?

Definitely self-investment. I'm a huge fan of filling your own cup first. Fill it to overflowing and then we can truly be better at everything - creating, earning and giving back.

My key take-outs

Lea's approach is certainly unique in the financial planning world. I know of very few firms who have taken a 'one to many' approach and offer webinars and retreats as a way of connecting with clients. I also love that she caters to those who are interested in the whole person philosophy, and putting their health and wealth together. The idea of creating a social enterprise with financial services is pretty new and creating profit and value for herself and her clients makes great sense.

Offering scholarships for women, especially those leaving abusive relationships, is a fabulous give back and a great resource for those who don't know where to turn when rebuilding their lives.

Lea's niche approach also caters to the more recent generations who have grown up knowing nothing but social media and the internet. It might seem a bit strange to others who've grown up forging trusted 'face-to-face' relationships with the professionals we trust with our money, but it's certainly working for her and her audience.

I also love Lea's thought process in asking if her future self will appreciate what she's now doing with her money. It's a question we can also ask ourselves before any discretionary purchase. It will make us much more aware of whether what we're buying is really necessary.

And how much sense does it make to fill your own cup first so that we can better serve others? Such a great analogy!

> In order to manage money well, we need to manage ourselves well.
>
> Lea Schodel

David Braithwaite

Citrus Financial, UK

'You control your money; it shouldn't control you. Understand it and don't be frightened of money.'

@CitrusDavid

David Braithwaite is the sole director of Citrus Financial, based in Hildenborough, outside London, and has ownership or part-ownership in four other related businesses – Citrus Healthcare, Citrus Accountancy, Citrus Conveyancing and Citrus Wills and Trusts.

David regularly appears on various television and radio programs, providing expert opinion and comment. His 'no nonsense' plain-English approach to explaining what can be complex financial matters is highly sought after.

TV appearances include those for BBC One, BBC World, BBC News 24, BBC News channel, ITV, BBC Breakfast, and BBC Watchdog. David was also the savings and investments expert for BBC2's Working Lunch program, and travels the country each year with the BBC when they put on financial roadshows.

David has appeared on BBC Radio 5 live, BBC Radio 2, Radio 4, BBC Scotland, BBC Sussex and BBC Southern Counties. He is also an international keynote speaker, appearing at the MDRT Annual Meeting in Northern America, Canada and Ireland, and on a National Roadshow in both Australia and New Zealand.

For over 15 years, David has also been the financial expert for BBC Radio Kent, where he has a regular slot each Saturday morning as well as commenting throughout the week on other topical financial stories that affect the British public, taking part in live phone-ins and commenting on the Budget. His regular Saturday morning appearances tackle the questions people want answered, one subject at a time.

I first crossed paths with David when he was invited to be a guest speaker at the National Conference of the Association of Financial Advisers (AFA) in Cairns, Australia, in October, 2015. Unfortunately, I wasn't able to make the event but we connected on Twitter. I then met David at the Vancouver Million Dollar Round Table (MDRT) event in June 2016, where he was a main platform speaker, delivering his presentation 'My balloon was about to burst – is yours?' We caught up a few times with colleagues during the event, managed to stay in touch via social media and met up again in Orlando, Florida, at the 2017 MDRT conference.

David describes his background as very normal and about as average as it can get. Family included mum, dad (both teachers) and a younger sister. He remembers that they never lacked anything - all the basics of life were always there. They lived in an average three-bedroom home and enjoyed a modest lifestyle. They travelled locally within the UK for their holidays with no international trips as a family.

Only later did he realise that sometimes life may have been a bit of a struggle, with his parents occasionally needing assistance from their own parents.

Sadly, David's sister developed breast cancer and passed away at 35, leaving her husband behind and, naturally, quite a hole in the family. David's answers to my questions expand on this background, his journey to become a financial advisor and how he approaches this role. You can also find out more from David via @CitrusDavid.

From my parents, it was probably that if you want something badly enough, you'll make it happen. I got quite tall very early and outgrew my pushbike by the time I was 15 and desperately wanted a new racer. My parents offered me a very different model to what I wanted and so I decided I'd rather go without than settle for less than what I wanted.

After they had a rethink, they took me back to another bike shop and allowed me to choose what I wanted. But it came with a lesson: I had to work for it. They put the price of the bike at the top of a chart and every time I did jobs and chores around the house, like cleaning the car, I'd work off part of the price of the bike. When they moved recently, they found the receipt for the bike [included below] and had it framed for me. I still have it in my office, and love what that taught me. There were no handouts. You had to go out and do things to make them happen. I also worked a paper route and in a kitchen early Saturday morning, leaving to then work the day in an electrical retailer to supplement my income.

But it was probably my grandfather who was the canniest about money. He was in sales and totally had the gift of the gab. When he semi-retired, he worked in a car dealership and had access to cars that would come in with low mileage from older drivers that he could pick up at a good price. He made a deal with me that we'd be partners. I was around 18 or 19 at the time. He'd pick up the car for us, I'd do it up with a clean and detail, polish and a refurbish and we'd resell it at a higher price. We'd deduct expenses I'd laid out in parts or products, and split the difference 50/50. There were still no handouts for me. It was strictly business and taught me some great lessons.

P. W. EVERNDEN

47 MAIDSTONE ROAD,

PADDOCK WOOD, KENT

TN12 6DG

Telephone PADDOCK WOOD 2823

New and Reconditioned Cycles

Accessories & Repairs

AGENT FOR ALL CYCLES

17.12. 1983

MR BRAITHWAITE

VAT Reg. No. 205 1687 89

25" raleigh Stratos 10 £ 135·28

NE 307869⁴

Bal. £ 135·28

I was one of those kids who didn't like school. I certainly don't look back at my school days and reminisce about how they were the greatest years of my life. I went to an all-boys school and wasn't interested in football and didn't really get the point of it all. I never had a vision or knew what I wanted to be when I grew up.

At one point, my parents were choosing my subjects for me and, even though I wasn't particularly interested, I did still challenge them on why I needed certain subjects. I asked my father why maths would be relevant in my life, and English studies and chemistry. If he couldn't prove to me why I'd need it, or how it would be relevant going forward, I wasn't interested. I didn't see the point of university either and certainly wasn't great at taking exams.

I was allowed to leave school when I was around 16 on the condition that I got a job. I applied for two jobs – one as a management trainee for a bank and the other as a stockbroker. I chose being a stockbroker, but after an eight-hour day, then a meal break and then compulsory overtime on top of another five hours per day, I was pretty disillusioned. I didn't want the life my manager was living; there was nothing aspirational in that and there was really no life outside of the office. Again, I didn't really feel that I fitted in or see the point of it all, so I left.

I then became a real estate agent and absolutely loved that job. I loved everything about buying and selling houses and saw value in adding a mortgage service for clients. Unfortunately, I ended up losing that job when the business went bust, but it set me on the path to where I am now.

One of my former colleagues there decided to go out on his own and I joined him in his mortgage business. This started me on the journey to self-employment and eventually setting up Citrus Financial.

Have you ever had any financial or personal setbacks?

Yes – when I was made redundant, I'd just gotten married and had signed up for my first mortgage. It was hardly an ideal start. My wife and I had one car between us and she was using it for work so it was difficult for me to get to interviews and I ended up taking unemployment benefits for six months.

That really forced me to take stock and I ended up partnering with a friend and selling electrical goods, accessories and computer consumables at car boot sales to make ends meet. It worked!

Some years later, my marriage broke down and I had to buy my wife out of our property on divorce. I was in a better position to do that by then, but I had taken on more debt than I really wanted.

Personally, there was also a time when I was suffering from a lot of stress and anxiety. It was a very tough time emotionally. I often wanted to give everything up and felt unworthy of the position I found myself in. I found having a trusted and supportive network a great blessing and now include this part of my life in keynote addresses around the world. It's surprising how these feelings resonate with so many people and they want to share their stories too. I really think we need to live in a world where we make it safe to be vulnerable with each other and share what's really going on for all of us. We're all in this together.

What's the best financial advice you've ever been given?

You have to take the odd risk. Be aware first, do your research and make sure it's calculated, and then head into it with a can-do attitude. If you work hard enough and have passion about what you do, you'll find a way to get things done. Then, the money will come.

What's your top financial tip for others?

Firstly, be aware of your monthly spend. You control your money; it shouldn't control you. Understand it and don't be frightened of money.

Do you have a message you'd like your son, Harvey, to learn about money?

I'd like him to learn positive messages about money, that delayed gratification is important and about the value of things versus the cost. He's currently interested in opening a bank account and is learning that you have to work in exchange for money. I'd like him to know that it costs so many hours of work to purchase goods, like an iPad and, if it breaks, it can't just be easily replaced. That takes more time and effort.

He was sitting in his den recently looking out on a reserve by our home and turned to me and commented, 'We're very lucky, aren't we?' That was a really nice moment.

Do you run a family budget?

Yes, I do, I run all of it. My partner isn't great with money. We take out of my business what we need as a monthly wage. We have a comfortable life and I'm very aware of what our needs are but most of my funds are retained in my business.

Do you do business planning and budgeting?

Yes, each of my five businesses is a self-contained unit and needs to support itself. We compare historical results and run forecasts. I use spreadsheets and know exactly what the business needs to make ends meet on a monthly basis.

I also invest in a professional development program, Strategic Coach, and utilise the '3 Buckets' method, so we always know what's pending, what's in the pipeline and what's paid. It's a simple method that means we always know what's outstanding and what needs following up.

Citrus Accounting uses Xero for our clients, but we mostly prefer spreadsheets in-house.

Do you use any financial apps?

Personally, no. Aside from internet banking, I don't use any other software for financial management.

From a straight financial perspective, in the UK we have access to tax-free investments and I highly recommend these to my clients.

Personally, you can never spend too much on your own education. I'm very interested in leaving a legacy and want to ensure that every person who crosses my path is better off by speaking with me.

I invest heavily in my own education with ongoing personal development with Strategic Coach and connecting with colleagues and sharing ideas at the MDRT events.

I also like to give back and act in a volunteer position as the governor at a local school, ensuring the health and safety of the students.

When possible, we also like to sponsor our clients who are involved in various charitable works that are important to them.

My key take-outs

David's tip to not be afraid of money really struck a chord with me. I don't think many people even realise that they are afraid of money. Sometimes the things we don't understand confuse us or cause fear, so it's an interesting question to confront – am I afraid of money?

I also love that David is open and vulnerable to sharing his journey with anxiety too. I know it's been lovely for him to hear feedback when he's spoken at events and I was privileged to hear an advisers' response when meeting with him at MDRT, and hear the impact David's story had on him. We definitely need to live in a world where it's safe to be able to share what we're going through and be able to reach out for help when it's needed. It's amazing what can come back to us when we're brave enough to admit we're struggling – first to ourselves, and then to others.

In many families, money isn't spoken about and positive lessons around finance are rarely passed on so now is a great time to start forging new habits in your own family. Taking calculated risks is also an interesting one. We're not talking about gambling, but weighing the pros and cons. Sometimes we'll kick some goals, other times we won't, but I'd rather try and fail than succeed at doing nothing.

I also love Harvey's gratitude. How awesome that at seven he's already taking the time to be grateful. Sometimes, just realising how fortunate we are and being grateful for what we have can leave us in a better place. There's always going to be people both better off and worse off than we are, so being thankful for what we have is a very important lesson.

And investing in ourselves and our ongoing education is also something I really resonate with. I completely believe that the day I stop learning is the day I'm likely to cock up my toes, so self-education is always very important to me.

> For it matters not, how much we own, the cars, the house, the cash,
> What matters is how we live and love and how we spend our dash.
>
> Linda Ellis (for the full poem see www.linda-ellis.com/the-dash-the-dash-poem-by-linda-ellis-.html)

Doug Bennett

DB Financial, UK

'Always put aside 15 per cent of your income for the future. Each pay packet is really to provide for two people.'

@DB_Financial

Doug Bennett is a mortgage broker and financial adviser who has worked in the financial services industry since 1983. Over the years, he has arranged over 2000 mortgages and has a wealth of experience in this area. Recently, he has also moved his business into the corporate protection, personal retirement and investment planning arena to ensure his clients receive a holistic view of their situation.

Apart from being a really bad golfer, Doug enjoys relaxing with a good book. He's also managed to ride a 500cc Royal Enfield motorcycle in the Himalayas and completed a trek up Kilimanjaro. He has also completed the London Marathon and raises money for local charity Us in a Bus. Doug speaks at industry seminars and events to provide motivation and guidance to other advisers within the planning industry. Doug and his wife, Bonnie, live in Crawley, in the UK. Doug runs DB Financial and has two adult sons.

I was fortunate enough to meet Doug at the Vancouver MDRT Meeting in June 2016, where he presented his focus session on how he came back from almost financial oblivion.

Personally, Doug is the oldest of four siblings. His father was a long-serving member in the armed forces before changing careers and starting work as a police officer. Doug's mother worked part-time as a cashier in a garage to supplement the family income in between raising the children. As the oldest, Doug felt that weighty expectations were placed upon him, with his mother hopeful he'd become the managing director of a large multi-national corporation. He did manage to win a scholarship to university; however, he failed the entrance exams and that finished his university career.

At no stage does Doug remember any direct lessons from his family or school about money, except that there didn't ever seem to be much.

Sadly, Doug's father passed away at age 64 within months of his mother, aged 63, which naturally caused a big shift in how he viewed his own future and possible longevity. His answers to my questions are below and you can follow Doug via @DB_Financial.

I had no formal or informal education on how to manage money. I worked for a building society and then become a mortgage broker in 1988, and learned many lessons about money first-hand by helping clients manage their own personal finances, budgets and mortgages.

Sadly, yes. After my parents passed away and we finalised probate and settled the estate and distributions to my siblings, my wife and I decided to purchase a new and larger home. We were fortunate in that we could keep our existing home and rent out that property. The timing, however, was less than ideal with the global financial crisis (GFC) striking within months.

The fallout of the GFC was profound and my business suffered a lot. We went from writing around 10 to 15 mortgages a month, plus arranging associated protection with insurance policies, to around 25 per annum, meaning my business income took a huge dive, and we had the additional debt to service.

We ended up renting out rooms to pilots for additional income because we're close to a major airport, even hiring out our driveway for parking fees. Credit cards became maxed out and we were really struggling.

Thankfully, I was able to invest in my own professional development and in business learnings through organisations like Strategic Coach and the Million Dollar Round Table, and slowly but surely managed to trade through this really difficult time. I was emotionally low and not sure which way to turn but I'd met some great people through my business networks and they displayed confidence in my abilities, which, in turn, allowed me to be able to pick up and turn things around.

Doug Bennett

The idea that Paul Armson came up with really resonated with me, known as the 'Bucket Strategy', which is great for people starting off on their financial planning journey.

Your bucket is your liquid cash – what's available and accessible – in your bank or wallet. Your water level in the bucket is your available 'liquid' funds, like your bank account, savings or investment and share accounts, and it's topped up regularly by your income, interest and dividends.

Assets like your home, investment properties, business or pension savings aren't in your bucket, because they're not readily available cash or liquid assets. Perhaps one day, they'll become liquid (when sold) and can then be used to top up your bucket.

The bucket has taps that come out of it that drain money. At the moment, the tap is likely your current expenditure, lifestyle needs including groceries, utilities and living expenses. In the future, it could be desired expenditure in retirement. There are also one-off needs like when we replace the car or the fridge and, possibly later, long-term aged care needs. All put a drain on our bucket.

Our water level can either run out early or we could overflow and have too much money. That may not sound like an issue, but it can create tax bills, or mean that you haven't lived as well as you could have while you were able.

Financial planners can assist you in working out how much to put away or spend and control the flows from your bucket. I thought that was a great way to describe what planners do and how they can assist their clients.

Your top financial tip?

Always put aside 15 per cent of your income for the future. Each pay packet is really to provide for two people. You need to look after your current self, but also provide for your future self, the one you're going to become.

The statistics show that we'll either become an old person, possibly a disabled one, or dead. Having saved 15 per cent of our wages will help provide in all scenarios. We can utilise the funds for life insurance (to provide a legacy for our families when we die), income protection (to replace our income should we become disabled) or fund our retirement pension (to enable us to live comfortably as we age).

What have you passed on to your sons about money?

Thankfully, my son Jason has embraced the 15 per cent rule and puts away into his pension fund regularly.

Jake started out with a part-time job, now working full-time, and is a total hoarder. He saves more than anyone I know, including me. I'm pleased that they both take their financial futures seriously.

Do you have a personal budget? Do you recommend one to your clients?

Yes, we run a family budget; they're very important and I work closely with my clients to ensure that they also manage their funds well.

When I meet with young couples, I always suggest that they keep separate bank accounts. It's very important to maintain independence. However, I also ensure we work through joint expenses that need to be shared like rent or mortgages, food and utility bills. I then suggest a joint bank account that both contribute to, to manage these expenses every week or pay cycle. That way, all expenses are always covered and what remains can be spent, invested or saved.

How do you manage your business finances?

I don't have any software that we use but I'm very aware of my cash flow and what's required in outgoings each month. We run spreadsheets and I monitor these a couple of times each week.

What do you see as the biggest benefits to clients for using a financial adviser?

I've really enjoyed transitioning from financial adviser, working more in the product selling space to financial planner and being involved in people working towards their goals. I'm a big fan of lifestyle financial planning and haven't met any clients yet who haven't benefited from that. We get very involved in our clients' financial lives and know that they're thinking about the education we provide before they make purchases. We end up becoming a 'giver of permission', which is a great position of trust.

We also act as a coach over time. I liken the investment experience to learning to swim. First, we go for a paddle, then we might learn to swim, move on to snorkelling, and then scuba-diving or even deep-sea dives. It's a process of steps and we all find where we're comfortable with sitting – and investing is very similar. It's best to start conservatively by having a paddle, and then build up our confidence before taking on more risk.

We have a 'no diving allowed' policy for newer clients, meaning that they can't jump in at the deep end until they gain some experience and confidence first. So, we act as coaches along the way, and I think that's of great benefit to clients.

What's your favourite form of investment?

Once, I thought I added value to my clients by building portfolios and choosing what we thought were the best investments, mostly based around past performance. As it turns out, that's not where I add value, so now I utilise preset planning models from a large fund manager and we outsource the investment philosophy entirely. These are low-cost funds that suit most clients based on their current life stages.

I'm more interested now in having my clients invest in their own personal experiences such as saving to meet goals like a home or travel, rather than fund picking.

I also invest heavily in my own professional development to continue to be able to give my clients a great experience. I'd rather be interested, than interesting.

My key take-outs

I totally love that Doug was able to pick himself up, dust himself off, and start all over again … as the song goes! Most of us find ourselves in financial straits that are less than ideal at some point in our lives, but it's our mindset and attitude in being able to work through those times that breeds resilience, and I love that he now shares that story with colleagues from around the world. It's also interesting how much our own confidence is affected by our situation, so it's a great time to find a cheer squad. Surround yourself with people who believe in you and can highlight your strengths and encourage you, even when you're not in a place to see those qualities yourself.

I enjoyed learning about the bucket strategy too. It's a really simple way of looking at money that makes a lot of sense. While we work, we're filling our bucket but, as we know, those taps are draining it along the way! How will we manage the top ups and the taps?

Doug's idea for new couples about maintaining independence while sharing expenses is also a great tip, especially for those entering new relationships.

I also like the idea of investing for two people – our current self and our future self. It's a great tip! And finally, I'm all about investing in experiences too. From scuba-diving, hiking to motorbike riding, I want to try so many different and new things! You don't hear of too many people on their deathbed mourning the things they did do - rather, they mourn all the opportunities they missed, along with spending more time with their families and friends, and being more adventurous!

If someone asked you, could you die happy today, how would you answer? Have you done lots of things you wanted to? Do you want to spend time reconnecting with loved ones? Do you still have lots ahead? It may sound morbid, but it certainly tends to refocus us on what really counts in our lives.

Action cures fear.

David J Schwartz

Success leaves clues.

Tony Robbins

Jenny Brown

CEO JBS Financial Strategists

'Just start. There's never going to be a perfect time, but get started.'

@JBSFinancialJB

Jenny Brown is the award-winning CEO and Founder of JBS Financial Strategists, a boutique financial planning company in Melbourne. She's proudly the 2013 AFA Financial Adviser of the Year and the FS Smileys Scholar of the Year, together with being the Australian Chair of MDRT.

Jenny offers more than 25 years' experience in the financial planning industry, where her personal philosophy has never wavered – she gets to know what's important to her clients first, and then acts to help them achieve their dreams. Specifically, she helps create and manage wealth strategies. Her business is about building relationships, which has enabled her to grow JBS into the thriving and progressive practice it is today, backed by a lively and dedicated team of advisers and specialists.

I first met Jenny on Twitter! So, you can't tell me social media doesn't work for meeting new, wonderful and very real people! We were a couple of a handful of financial advisers who had embraced social media for our financial planning businesses within Australia and she reached out to connect.

It wasn't long before we both found ourselves at an event designed to encourage more advisers to use social media for their businesses and we finally met in person and have been friends ever since, often crossing paths at conferences and events. We also met up again when industry journal Financial Standard ran annual awards for social advisers and we both made the Digital Dozen and the #FSPower50 – awarded to the top 50 most influential advisers in Australia in the financial space.

Jenny and I are very active in both the Association of Financial Advisers and the Million Dollar Round Table in volunteer roles, and even though we live over 1,700 kilometres apart, we still manage to find ourselves meeting up a few times each year at various conferences. (Jenny lives with her husband, Brendan, on the Mornington Peninsula in Victoria.)

Life at JBS is all about having fun too, and Jenny invests heavily in her team to ensure happy campers all round. Her great passions are social media and networking, but she's equally *driven to help women in business and sits on several business advisory boards.*

Jenny's background, like many of those featured in this book, is also very working class. Her parents were a bit older when they had her (Dad being 40 with Mum 28) and she is the eldest of two, her brother being four-and-a-half years younger.

Dad worked in advertising for many years, selling space in large Australian media corporations like Channel 10 and Channel 7 before heading out on his own to freelance in the same area. Her mother worked as the executive assistant to the chairman of radio station 2UE before retiring from the workforce to raise their family in the 1960s. Dad was always the family breadwinner.

Jenny's family never really talked about money, as seems to be another theme in this book. It wasn't hidden, but it wasn't talked about either. Her father was a World War II veteran whose parents had survived the Great Depression and, in consequence, he knew the value of things. Nothing was ever handed out on a silver platter and working hard for what you got was a must. A family expression Jenny remembers fondly is 'money doesn't grow on apple trees'. The family at that time lived in a pear and apple orchard area, so it seemed fitting enough. If you wanted something, you needed to work for it. Pocket money wasn't a given, but needed to be earned through doing chores around the house.

Larger spends like a new bike were subsidised by Christmas or birthday funds, but half still had to be earned. Delayed gratification and working hard for what you got were just how things were done. It was about instilling the right ethos without the handout mentality that seems a little more pervasive today.

Jenny has never had any major financial setbacks but has made a few investments that certainly haven't turned out or delivered as intended.

So, here are Jenny's answers to the questions I've been posing, and you can catch up with her via @JBSFinancialJB.

How did you become a financial planner?

Basically, I fell into financial planning. I'd followed my father into advertising but was made redundant in the 'recession we had to have' in Australia (according to then-treasurer Paul Keating) in the early 1990s. Everyone was being laid off, so I couldn't get work in advertising again.

I answered an ad in the paper for a sales role, and managed to find myself selling insurance for what was then Norwich Union. Over time, I came to understand more about how insurance fits into overall financial planning and some years later joined a large financial planning firm in Melbourne as an independent adviser – the Bongiorno Group – which gave me a great grounding in the industry.

Since then, working on my own, I have built up JBS Financial Strategists over the past 25 years.

What's the best financial tip you've ever been given?

Well, it was probably from my mentors at Bongiorno's, some years ago and in the very early days of starting financial planning. I was commuting over an hour to work each way, every day, and he eventually said to me, 'You need to live where your clients are living.' It made sense to me, and so I sold my home and moved closer to town, and to where my clients were living in Glen Iris, Victoria.

He might as well have said 'location, location, location' because that's what it really boiled down to. The values of homes in the area I moved from, compared to where I moved to when I finally sold were immeasurably different. It was a good lesson.

I've recently sold that home in Glen Iris and a holiday home in Sorrento to make a lifestyle choice to move to Mount Martha on the Mornington Peninsula in Victoria, southern Australia, with my husband and dogs. I sat down and did the sums on the sale of the homes and weighed up the pros and cons and financials and it was just right for us. It's been something we've looked forward to for a while and we absolutely love our new home.

I also learned a good lesson on how important it is for our investments to keep up with inflation, based on my maternal grandfather's experience. He was a chief accountant at East Oil (now Mobil), and retired on a fixed non-indexed pension. Unfortunately, without inflation, it devalued every year of his retirement.

Do you have a top financial tip that you like to give clients?

Yes, absolutely. Just start. There's never going to be a perfect time, but get started. Don't worry if it's too late or too early; you have to start somewhere, so do it now.

Also, I'm a big believer in asking for help. If you want something, don't be afraid to ask.

I also agree with the tenets that my parents laid down about teaching children the right lessons about money. We grow up in a world where we can have it all, and now. Kids need to know that it takes time and effort to earn things. Teach them early that it takes hard work to get ahead, and get the right advice early.

Do you have a personal budget? Do you recommend one to your clients?

Yes, we do. Making sure the set expenses are taken care of is really important. All fixed bills are covered first and then we both have funds that are for our personal use.

If I want to buy clothes or makeup, it doesn't impact on the family budget. If I don't have the funds to do that, then I go without, or wait until I have the personal spending money again.

I talk to clients about doing the same thing – that is, ensuring all the bills are covered first. Whether you do that with a joint account or bills account or just pay half each, go with whatever works for your family. Just make sure everything is covered before you spend on discretionary needs.

Do you run business plans and forecasts?

Yes, annually each financial year, we take stock and look at what's happened and plan for the coming 12 months. Every quarter we also review what's happened and see if we need to make adjustments for the coming quarter.

What do you see as the biggest benefits to clients for using a financial adviser?

Well, I like to use the analogy that even elite athletes use the services of a coach. There's always something we can learn and it's the same when it comes to our finances. To me it makes sense that people have a money coach. We can't know it all and it's really valuable to have someone you can use as a sounding board to bounce ideas off and see what makes sense.

We can evaluate good and bad investments, superannuation and trusts, and the pros and cons for an individual's needs.

Another great benefit is that advisers sit you down and make you articulate your goals. Most people don't have a plan. We often have a broad idea of where we'd like to be, but nothing really concrete about how we're going to get there. That's where we add the real value. We keep you accountable.

Do you have a favourite form of investment?

My personal preferences are for property and blue chip shares, especially for the long term. But everyone is different so you need to do what's right for your individual circumstances. A diversified portfolio that provides the right mix for you to reach your goals is vital.

My key take-outs

I totally love the idea of delayed gratification. Everything truly seems that much sweeter when we've had to wait that little bit longer or work that little bit harder to achieve it. It's not always an easy lesson to learn, but one that's certainly worth it. I believe it also truly grows our appreciation for items.

I also like ideas that are contrarian to others that have become mainstream. An idea that has been bandied around for a long time has been to 'pay yourself first', yet Jenny suggests making sure all fixed expenses are covered first. Which way do you lean? If living week to week, you may not have a choice, but it's worth assessing which camp you're in. Both can work, but making it work is up to you!

I also love that you should view your financial adviser as your coach. If you use a personal trainer for your body or a business coach to get ahead, it makes perfect sense to engage a money coach to keep you financially accountable.

I'm also seeing a theme that all the financial professionals so far run budgets for both their business and personal lives. Perhaps another great lesson to take on board?!

> If you don't ask, the answer is always no.
>
> Nora Roberts

Erin Truscott

GCA Financial Services

'Learning basic financial literacy
is so important. Know what you
are and aren't capable of.'

@Erin_Truscott

Erin Truscott is a financial adviser and shareholder of GCA Financial in Brisbane. She spends her days working with her clients to help them build meaningful strategies to achieve their lifestyle goals, with a true belief that wealth is far more than just money. Before joining GCA, Erin spent eight years as a practice development manager, advising practices to help develop their businesses, work better with their clients and, in turn, prosper alongside them. This was where Erin found her true passion for advice and knew she needed to do more, to ensure she could help as many Australians as possible to get better advice with meaningful outcomes. Since purchasing a share in her business, Erin hasn't looked back, and is excited to be part of our ever-evolving financial services industry.

You know how sometimes you have those people in your life who seem to have always been there? Well, I'm pretty sure the amazing Erin is one of those. I have no clear memory now of how we met, but we've crossed paths for many years at industry events and conferences, and finally Erin moved away from business development manager–land and into advising herself.

These days, we both serve on the AFA Inspire committee for Queensland and love giving back to this fabulous industry we both work in. Together, we've arranged events designed to allow women in financial services to connect and be mentored via Bubbles & Troubles networking events, arranged wellness mornings and supported International Women's Day, among many other events.

Erin is a bit of a rock star, and recently took out the AFA Rising Star Award, given to celebrate excellence in the next generation of financial advisers who have been practicing for three years or fewer. She's currently expecting her first baby and we can't wait to welcome her gorgeous girl into the world.

Her answers follow, and you can catch her via @Erin_Truscott.

What was family life like when growing up?

When my parents got together, they already had three sons between them, and then had my sister and me together. Dad most often worked as a building foreman and Mum was an interior designer. Dad usually also had something else running on the side, and was very interested in health and wellness projects. They were very entrepreneurial and I learned a lot by watching them. Of their five children, four of us run our own businesses now. What I really did notice was that we'd often have times of plenty and times when things were tight, which is pretty standard with building trades. It was very 'stop, start'. I'd watch them invest time and energy and money into projects and they wouldn't always work out. But there was always the underlying lesson that you just keep trying and don't give up.

Where did you learn about money?

Probably from the school of life. Mum and Dad were much more focused on life skills. Receiving a higher education wasn't something that was highly recommended in my family and I remember that sometimes, during the leaner times, we couldn't afford new uniforms or books or shoes for the new year during our schooling. We had to make do with what we had and that teaches you too that there aren't always times of abundance.

We all worked hard from a very young age, starting with part-time jobs as soon as we could. I also remember looking up to my uncle who was a doctor and thinking of him as being highly successful. They had five girls, a nice house with a trampoline in the front and a swimming pool in the back. I remember that as being, in my head, the definition of being successful from working hard.

How did you become a financial adviser?

I'd saved hard and gone to work in London and got a job as a temp. I worked in finance-related roles for big corporations like Audi and BMW and loved the numbers. I really liked the work.

When I came back to Australia, I started work with Professional Investment Services, a licensee that supports financial advisers, assisting the Head of Research. From there, I moved on to become a business development manager and then a practice development manager supporting advisers within their businesses. It was here that my love of advice was born. I worked with a lot of different advisers and practices and got to see firsthand the difference they could make in their clients' lives and knew that that was what I wanted to do to. Eventually, I left management and began to work with one of the practices I'd formerly assisted. It was a big adjustment to go from a great salary to almost starting over, but I knew it was where I wanted to be. The plan was for me to become a partner in the business, which meant a lower starting salary and a major lifestyle adjustment, but it's all been worth it.

Have you had any financial setbacks?

I had a lot of fun when I was younger and I spent, just not even thinking about the future. I guess I figured it would all take care of itself. I was never focused on a budget or setting aside money for the 'rainy day.' When I went onto that lower salary, it was a real adjustment for me. I had to use all of the very limited resources I had to make ends meet. I didn't have a safety net and that required a big mindset change for me. I guess it wasn't really a financial setback but it sure made me shift focus and is why I now love helping young people to change focus and make sure they don't make the same mistakes I did.

What's the best financial advice you've been given?

I think it's around being accountable. Although I'm an adviser myself now, I still work with my original financial adviser. We get together regularly to talk about my goals and I love checking in with her. She definitely keeps me on track and focused and reminds me to hold myself accountable.

What's your top financial tip?

I'm a big believer in not spending beyond your means. Learning basic financial literacy is so important. Know what you are and aren't capable of. Money worries are a stress and burden that can affect our lives well into the future, and if you're not good at it, seek professional help.

The other thing I like to tell people is just start. It doesn't matter how much you start with but just get something going. The more you do, the better results you'll see and that really motivates you to just keep going. Knowing you're on top of your finances means one less thing to stress about.

What would you like to teach your (future) daughter about money?

Definitely to start early. My partner, Jock, has very limited financial literacy and we've had a lot of discussions around budgeting and saving and why they're important. Teaching your children early is a gift.

We'll be doing a piggy bank for sure. I'm not really all about the money, but more what it can do for you, what it can create and the value of money. Don't take it for granted. Nothing comes for free. She can learn from my mistakes and learn to budget much earlier, right from her first job. I'll have her saving 10 per cent from the beginning! It's only a small amount, but it sure adds up over time!

Erin Truscott

Do you run a family budget?

Yes, and we revisit it very regularly. Because I'm expecting our first child, there are a lot of additional expenses at the moment with medical bills and all that goes with becoming a parent. We want to be able to set funds aside for her needs from our budget and look at how we can put more aside in case of any emergencies.

We're revising this monthly at the moment and tweaking it regularly as things change. We've only recently combined our finances as we're about to become an extended family, and that's created new stories and discussions. Pooling funds has been good for us as it now seems to provide great options for the family.

Do you do budgeting and forecasting in your business?

Yes, definitely. GCA Financial has someone filling a bookkeeper/accounting role internally in the business full-time and their role is to help create budgets and ensure profitability, among all the other jobs that need to be done. Having someone in that role means when we sit down for monthly meetings, we know what position we're in to be able to grow our team and exactly where we're at. We're very careful with the firm's funds and have different structures in place for protection as well, including partnerships and shareholders agreements.

We all meet in May to set goals for the business for the coming year ahead too.

Do you have a favourite form of investment?

Yes, we heavily utilise managed funds within the business using a 'core' and 'satellite' approach so that we're well diversified across asset classes and sectors. I invest in the same manner as I do my clients. I've always believed in diversification and the old 'don't put all your eggs in one basket' ideology.

I also invest in my own personal development. I'd like to do more public speaking and have recently invested in a course to help me improve that.

I've also regularly participated in the bike rides for Hands Across the Water, cycling 800 kms in the Thai heat and humidity and raising at least $10,000 each time. I've done this trip a few times, and now adore spending time with the Thai children and love the 'soul food' that giving back to those less fortunate provides. The human aspect of what we can do is very important to me. I constantly find that the more I give back, the more I get out of anything that I do.

Do you see benefits for clients to partner with advisers?

Completely. Like I said, I still have a financial adviser and love that she keeps me accountable. It's what we do for our clients. The world is constantly changing and we need to know how to adapt. It's a complex place that we live in now, with lots of changes, and navigating that is hard. It's great to have someone to bounce ideas off and talk about different outcomes that can help us provide a better future for ourselves.

Having someone in your corner who is staying up to date with constant legislative changes is a great benefit. It means you don't have to be all over it.

My key take-outs

Although it's one of the first financial lessons many of us learn, Erin is one of the few so far to mention diversification and 'not putting all your eggs in one basket'. The idea of splitting investments across property, shares, managed funds, ETFs, cash and fixed interest and other investment styles is hardly new, and most see the benefit of investing this way. Through diversification, if one particular asset class has a bad year, you can then hope to make that up with better performing assets. It's a very traditional way to invest, yet not everyone still agrees it's the best way to go. Some believe that knowing and deeply understanding a particular type of investment, such as residential property, is a better way to go. What about you? Do you have a favourite that you stick with, rather than spreading risk?

I love that ET's been in budgeting and savings chats with her partner and has plans on how to educate baby Florence going forward. I also love that she invests personally the same way as she invests her clients' money. It's a great question to ask your financial professional: 'Do you also invest in the same products or utilise personally the strategies you arrange for your clients?'

> You can't change what happened.
> But you can still change what will happen.
>
> Sebastian Vettel

David Batchelor

The Wills & Trusts Group, UK

'Live on 70 per cent of whatever income you earn. That's all you get for now.'

@DSBatchelor
@SolidusTrusts

David Batchelor formed Wills & Trusts Independent Financial Planning, an Independent Financial Advice (IFA) practice based in Oxfordshire, in 1992. David joined the board of the Life Insurance Association (LIA) in 2000 and, upon becoming President, secured the merger of the Society of Financial Advisers (SOFA) with the LIA to create the Personal Finance Society (PFS), on which he served as a board member for three years.

As one of the first Chartered and Certified Financial Planners, David has spent time as a question writer for the Chartered Insurance Institute (CII) and as an examiner for the Institute of Financial Planners (IFP). At the same time, David has qualified for MDRT Top of the Table for 17 consecutive years.

David has published four books, with How to charge fees the right way becoming a bible on moving to fee charging following the Retail Distribution Review in the UK, with all profits from this book being donated to charity.

David and I first met at the Florida MDRT meeting in 2017. He had been a speaker for some time and I had seen him present '60 Sales Ideas that Work – in 60 Minutes' with another adviser in Philadelphia three years earlier. Among other UK colleagues, including David, Doug and Michelle, we were introduced and met a few times socially throughout the course of the event, which is really where the true connections happen. Over a group dinner in Orlando one night we discussed our businesses and how we do things and found some similarities – and some huge differences.

I also attended a focus session David delivered called 'Sell and Manage 10× the Clients in 3 Days per Week' and his presentation of 'Triple your MDRT Results' during MDRT Speaks – where various advisers from around the world step up and provide a short presentation on what's working in their business or practical tips that other advisers can use.

David, too, was born into a very working-class family in south London. His father was a builder and his brother followed his father in the family business. David, however, became a

*professional drummer from ages 16 to 22 and would stand in
for percussionists and drummers at shows. He too became a
financial adviser by accident. After being offered a spot in the
band for the musical Starlight Express, with regular work for two
years ahead, he had to decide if he truly wanted to play exactly
what someone else decreed during 11 shows per week for a
very long time, or make a career change. He'd already gone for
a loan and been knocked back because he was a drummer with
irregular income, and so decided to take on a cashier's role in
a bank where the regular, although much less sexy, work was
likely to guarantee him a loan. He also decided that he enjoyed
playing too much to be pigeon-holed into playing something so
repetitively, despite the security, and still managed to play what
he liked part-time.*

*David had watched his father face bankruptcy twice, as is
sadly common in the building trade – in David's father's case
when he sub-contracted to a principal who went bust, and then
had a client who refused to pay. At 14 years old, he remembers
seeing the family car being repossessed and knew he never
wanted to be in a position where that could happen to him.*

*He knew from his father's experiences that in business 'cash
flow is king' and to never be reliant on just one customer. David
says his father was an incredibly generous man and always ready
to shout a round at the pub, though not a drinker himself, but had
no real concept of tomorrow. David also knew that his mother
was holding funds back to cover taxes and the hard times. His
mother was often the one who had to deal with the fallout of
having no money.*

*David now runs a few businesses, with Wills & Trusts Inde-
pendent Financial Planners being his main source of income.
A second business in which he has a 50 per cent stake is Solidus,
a document writing company that draws up legal documents
for use in his own business and offers services to other financial
advisers in a business-to-business space. After many requests
for mentoring, he has also set up an online training company to*

assist advisers in running their businesses and works as a coach one week per quarter for Strategic Coach in London, training other entrepreneurs.

In his spare time, David also has two bands – one is a five-piece jazz band that turns pop songs into jazz and the other is a 17-piece big band available for hire for weddings, festivals and private functions … and he has an 18-month-old son. Got to love an over-achiever! Here are his responses to my questions.

Where did you first learn about money?

Once I'd started working as a cashier for the bank, I started to understand a lot more about money. I then moved to an American bank, now known as Citibank, as a manager. I learned very quickly on the job and embraced their philosophy around the importance of the client rather than the product.

I also remember another influence from when I was at school, perhaps not about money but great lessons still, that I've implemented in my business. There was a teacher called Graham Baldwin. He was the sort of guy who got things done. The school had been trying to fundraise to complete a swimming pool for about 10 years and it was getting done, but extremely slowly. He decided the school should get a loan to finish it, but that wasn't allowed. So, he went and got a loan himself and had the school pay him back. The pool was finished and able to be used and the loan was repaid within three years.

He taught us about responsibility. If we wanted to go on a particular excursion, he'd allow it and then have us arrange it and make it happen. If we asked how to do something, he'd in turn ask, 'How would you do it?' He was a great teacher who was very much about getting things done and having us take leadership roles from an early age. He made us answer, 'What do you need to do to get where you want to go?' I still use some of those questions today, especially as an employer myself now.

How did you become a financial adviser?

After working for the bank for seven years, our remuneration structure was to be reorganised and the bonuses we then earned were to be redistributed, meaning I was going to take around a 30 per cent drop in my income. I decided I didn't want to stick around for that and I should start my own firm, which is where Wills & Trusts was born. I'd received a bequest of £9,000 from my grandmother's estate and used this to start my business.

I focused heavily on my own technical skills and was one of the first groups of advisers in the UK to achieve Chartered status. My business has also been among the pioneers to achieve Chartered status as a company, which we're very proud of. I have ensured that my team are all highly qualified and I'm pleased that every client-facing member of our team is very skilled at what they do.

Have you had any financial setbacks?

Yes, starting out in my own business was one of the most difficult times I've ever faced. My father thought I was crazy to leave the security of the bank role and start out on my own, especially due to the pay cut, and it certainly seemed that he was right in the first few years. Nan's money went very quickly and the clients I thought would beat a path to my door didn't.

I'd make 22 cold calls to clients before I'd get one appointment, and then I'd only convert one in three appointments to clients, meaning it took 66 calls to get each client. I was working late and then coming home to help my wife pack Valentine's cards so we'd have enough money to be able to afford nappies for our daughters. We ended up in around £50,000 debt while things were getting started.

The first three years were incredibly painful and very difficult. I learned about protecting the money that you had and the importance of cash reserves. I really didn't want to go the same way as my father and have to face bankruptcy.

Thankfully, after hours, days, weeks and years of hard work, the business became successful and we managed to trade through the hard times and repay the debt.

What's the best financial advice you've ever been given?

I'd learned early about personal development the importance of investing in yourself, and was introduced to 'how-to' books and become a bit addicted. I had no idea that you could learn from incredibly successful people and that they'd share their secrets with you. One of my favourites was *The Magic of Thinking Big* by David Schwartz. By this stage, I was also listening to Jim Rohn in the car on tape and was onto *The Art of Exceptional Living*. He had this theory on financial freedom that really resonated with me and I still use it to this day.

He advised to live on 70 per cent of whatever income you earn. That's all you get for now. Then, you save the other 30 per cent, but it's broken down into the following pots: 10 per cent is to go to long-term savings, the big stuff like replacing cars or housing deposits. The next 10 per cent is to go towards future financial independence and never to be touched. The remaining 10 per cent is to be split into half, with 5 per cent going to charities and the other 5 per cent to spend however you like and be completely enjoyed, guilt free – and it must be spent! It makes you feel so much better about the money you've saved. It's a great strategy and very effective.

What lessons have you passed on to your children about money?

My daughters are now 27 and 25 and I've taught them Jim Rohn's idea about the various pots and know that they use that. I know that by implementing that, they're also much more financially successful and savvy than many of their friends. Their friends have sometimes stumbled across how much they have in the bank and immediately planned a spending spree, but they've been told about money that's for saving and for spending. Not that they've then implemented it themselves.

Jack's still a bit too young for any of that right now.

Do you run a personal budget?

Yes, we also implement the same 'pots strategy' at home so regularly track that we're on target with that. My wife also runs her own business in PR with around 15 staff, so we get together monthly and run through the financials. I often highlight the importance of cash reserves again and making sure that there's enough aside that, if anything happens, we have enough to cover months', even years' worth of income as a buffer in case of the unexpected.

Do you run business plans and forecasting at work?

Yes, we run detailed plans for each business. Wills & Trusts has its original ten-year plan coming up in 2020 and we'll be working on another five-year plan to 2025. For Solidus, we're into a three-year plan.

We also ensure that we set aside 5 per cent of our funds for personal and professional development for me and the team to also invest in their growth. I personally invest in Strategic Coach each quarter and have been attending for around 19 years, and coaching with them in the UK for the past eight to nine years. Assisting other businesses helps keep me sharp. I also attend the MDRT annual meetings along with another Mastermind

Group called Vistage, which is a private advisory group that offers coaching, events and workshops, for a monthly meeting with other businesses.

We have a vision for our businesses, and a plan in place that supports the vision. I have a financial director now who runs forecasting for all the businesses and sets key performance indicators across the three of them. We make sure all areas are covered, which include reserves, cash in and out, performance versus budget, and potential business in the pipeline.

What benefits do you see in clients partnering with financial professionals?

Well, clients - like the rest of us - don't know what they don't know. It's easy to be influenced by the media, yet I've never met a wealthy journalist. We also advise our clients not to copy people who are poor. Many of our clients are already wealthy, but they're quite conservative with their funds. We're there to help them live life and learn to enjoy it.

I often run seminars for both new and existing clients and love sharing the story that it's only possible because of the bequest from my nan. That £9,000 she left me allowed me to start the firm that today they know and trust with their own wealth. It helps them to think differently too about their own estate planning and how they may like to leave their money. It totally changes the conversation.

Because of Nan, I now run regular public education seminars and can employ a team of people. We take care of the wealth of around 500 clients and manage around £250 million on their behalf. We also assist in managing around £2 billion for other advisers and their clients.

Our business motto is 'Protect, grow, enjoy' and we believe having fun is really important! I also have pinned to the wall the following statement that I came up with and look at every day: 'Design the plan, work the plan, and be prepared to change the plan when the enemy gets involved'.

My key take-outs

Well, I found David's career path into advice particularly fascinating. I can't say I've ever met anyone else who has gone from professional drumming into planning! Looking back, it's easy to determine those moments that change everything but, at the time, they can be a little harder to identify. I'm sure that walking away from the security of a two-year solid role in the music industry must have been difficult, especially to take on a secure and regular role in a bank, but it completely allowed David to meet his goals. He was able to get the loan he needed to get started because of the steady employment with a big firm, and still focus on playing the music he wanted to. Sounds like a 'win-win', although it may not have felt like that then.

And what a great story about being able to turn a small legacy into a thriving business. I'm sure Nan would be so proud! Making sure we address our estate planning needs is so important because I've seen firsthand the impact when a friend died. Even though he left a spouse and no children, settling the estate took around nine months due to complications and probate. Also, thinking outside the box and leaving a small legacy that can provide maximum impact to extended family is a great thing to consider.

I love David's lessons about being able to ignore the media who are only interested in bad news stories and would rather focus on the negative rather than the positive impacts that planners make in the lives of their clients every day.

Another pattern that seems to be emerging among both those in business and successful planners is their constant investment in personal development and ongoing learning. I'm looking forward to seeing future presentations of David's in the coming years.

> Everyone has a plan until they get punched in the face.
>
> Mike Tyson

Peita Diamantidis

Caboodle Financial Services

'Start using a debit card instead of a credit card so that you can only spend what you have.'

@Peitamd

Peita Diamantidis is a new form of 'geek' hybrid – maths and finance nerdiness combined with a passion for communicating that has her on a mission to empower the public to take charge of their finances.

With 20 years in the financial services industry, and the last 10 as a practising financial adviser, Peita has been most valued for her ability to take complex financial situations and break them down to their fundamentals. This culminated in the release of her first book Finance Action Hero: Basic Training in May 2014, with the follow-up Finance Action Hero: Mission Possible released in September 2016.

Utilising a background in actuarial studies (financial mathematicians who make accountants look hip and groovy), Peita has developed a keen interest in the science of 'applied innovation' – the adoption of innovative business models, development of innovative products and technologies, and engagement of the public in more innovative ways.

Strangely enough, Peita and I didn't cross paths at a financial planning industry event; instead, we met at ProBlogger (an annual conference for bloggers, held on the Gold Coast that year) a few years ago. By this stage, she'd already published her first book, and we'd connected on social media. Actually, the more you know about Peita, the more it probably makes perfect sense that we met at ProBlogger and not somewhere else …

Not long after, we were both privileged to be finalists in the AFA Female Excellence in Advice Awards, which is all about how the women in the advice world give back to women in their local societies, raising financial literacy levels and giving back to their communities. Gorgeous Peita won that year and was an incredibly deserving winner. She has gone on to deliver keynote speeches within the planning world and recently we worked together on various panel discussions hosted by Conexus in Sydney and Melbourne, covering opportunities for advisers and how to best tap in to those markets. As mentioned, she comes from an actuarial background and is a self-confessed math geek *and numbers nerd, but kindly leaves her cardigan at home on most occasions. We also both happen to be mad keen* Star Wars *fans, and she has a great laugh. So, what's not to love? Her answers to my questions follow, and you can also catch her via @Peitamd.*

What was family life like when you were growing up?

I lived something of a charmed life as a kid to be honest. We have a warm and fun family and we were all very involved in each other's interests, and so life was an exercise in the logistics of getting three kids around to soccer, tennis and dancing classes.

Dad was an executive in the insurance world and involved in IT for insurance companies and Mum was a homemaker who looked after us.

I went to a local public primary school on the North Shore of Sydney and then went to a private school for high school, and while we never wanted for anything growing up, in the school I went to, our family drove the Holden when most were driving BMW or Mercedes ... even a Lamborghini.

Where did you learn about money? What lessons did your parents teach you?

To be honest, and as geeky as it sounds, my first awareness of learning lessons about money was during my university days completing actuarial studies and then during my graduate position with a major bank on the money market floor and futures exchange. Nothing is like standing in 'the market' when a global economic event occurs to teach you lessons about the unpredictability and randomness of share markets.

Looking back, I don't have a conscious awareness of money lessons from my parents, or of many conversations about money at all.

How did you become a financial services professional?

I had a natural bent for mathematics as a kid – in fact, I am sure lots of my mates thought I was bent due to my geeky maths interests! Therefore, I naturally leant towards finance studies and then work in the finance sector.

My career started in investment banking and corporate finance, which was a baptism by fire into business, analysing value and understanding debt and tax structures. However, at its worst I could do well over 100 hours per week and so just prior to turning into a true corporate zombie I decided to take the skills I had developed and apply them in the financial advice industry – offering the same sort of advice, just to individuals rather than big corporates.

Have you had any financial setbacks?

Nothing like the sort of thing I witness as a financial adviser. Most of my historical financial challenges had to do with taking a while to learn basic positive financial behaviours. A good example was when I finished up in investment banking. I had been earning very good money for a number of years, but came out of it with nothing other than serious credit card debt. The more I earnt, the more I spent, and I did a lot of 'accidental' or 'lazy' spending that meant I burnt through lots of money without any actual recollection of what I had spent it on.

What is the best financial advice you've ever been given, and who was it from?

This was back in my investment banking days and was during the dotcom bubble in the late '90s. Most of my colleagues were chasing all the latest internet business deals and the buzz in the office was high. I had a meeting with a client who was a very successful investor in infrastructure businesses (think transport, health and so on) and, therefore, 'old school' compared to what my colleagues were chasing.

We were debating the manic rise of the dotcom businesses, and he said something that has stayed with me to this day: 'But where is the cash flow, Peita?'

You see, these businesses were seeing huge increases in their share market value, but actually had no revenue coming in. People were buying the shares based on potential alone, before they were really even businesses. Ultimately, they were going to have to pay staff and pay bills, and with no revenue coming in they would rapidly get themselves into trouble. Which is exactly what happened, and then their share prices tanked.

Cash is king, no matter how 'viral' your idea may be. And this is true for individuals as much as for businesses.

What is your top personal financial tip for others?

This is my version of the tip given to me: 'Spend less than you earn.' As obvious as this sounds, most people don't do this, or have no idea whether they do this. What it comes down to is making sure you understand exactly how much you earn, and then taking the time to be clear on exactly where the money goes. So many of us spend without thought, and are then surprised when we find ourselves in trouble. Cash is king, so make sure you know where your hard-earned money is going! Invariably the biggest hurdle to this is credit card spending so, if nothing else, I encourage people to start using a debit card instead of a credit card so they can only spend what they have.

Do you run a family budget?

My husband and I do not have an itemised budget; however, what we do have is an understanding of the normal level of excess we have per month - meaning, after bills and debt repayment, how much of the month's income we normally have left over. Therefore, whenever the month seems a bit thin, we go back through the expenses for the month and see if any bad habits or unnecessary spending has crept in. This isn't about restricting ourselves; it is merely making sure that anything we spend money on falls into the intentional spending category rather than accidental or lazy spending.

Do you run business forecasting and budgeting?

Monitoring your business numbers is fundamental. However, it is important to understand that they are simply a way of keeping score - of your progress in growing your revenue, or your ability to keep your expenses within certain limits.

The first and most important step is to build your vision for the year ahead - what projects do you want to implement and where do you hope to see the business growing and evolving over the year. Then you can come up with the forecasts for revenue and expenses that match that. When you do those forecasts, they should then give you a 'heads up' of any points where cash flow may be tight due to new projects or staff you need, which can therefore enable you to come up with a plan way ahead of time to deal with that. Plans come first, budgets come second.

Do you use any financial apps?

No, not presently, but we are reviewing the available offerings and hope to have something to offer our clients in the future in that space.

Like anything in life, I am a big fan of trying to learn enough to be dangerous, and then bringing in the experts for the heavy lifting. Therefore, I encourage everyone to get to understand their money behaviours, find out where all their different accounts are, and get comfortable enough to ask loads of questions about all the different facets of their financial life.

The idea here is to know enough to be able to tell when they need help, and then determine which of the two types of expertise they need:

- *a technical expert* – a full on financial geek who can crunch those numbers for them and help them make better decisions in the future

- *a coaching expert* – someone who has seen loads of people just like them and can give insight into the mistakes people often make and lean them towards the path of success.

Laughter! There is simply nothing better for the soul, the heart or the mind than a good session of belly laughter. I can remember so many times in the past when things felt overwhelming or I simply couldn't get my head around how to solve a major challenge I was facing, and I either caught up with some of my troublemaker friends or even went to a comedy gig and the resulting laughter cleared my mind and lifted my energy levels. Solutions immediately presented themselves and I was back on track.

Laughter isn't something that happens accidentally, however; you need to recognise the need for it and make sure to make it part of your life, and invest as frequently as possible!

My key take-outs

Realising cash is king and spending less than you earn both make a comeback here, and also happen to be two favourites of mine.

Moving from credit cards to debit cards makes a lot of sense to avoid that 'lazy' or invisible spending. So often, it's easy to just put something on credit and, by the time the bill comes in, not even remember that we've done it. PayPass or Tap and Go spending options are also causing grief for people because they make spending now so easy – with having to worry about being accountable coming later.

Moving from vision first and to budget later is also a great idea. It's so important to set those big picture goals and work out how to get there.

And who doesn't need a reminder to have a laugh? For so many, money or finance can be as dry as it gets and remembering to enjoy life along the way is a great tip to reset, refresh and be reminded to move on.

Also, being able to work out whether you need a technical expert or a finance coach is a great tip. It puts you totally in the driver's seat when deciding which type of adviser you need to deal with.

> *Vivian:* The stores are not nice to people. I don't like it.
> *Edward:* Stores are never nice to people.
> They're nice to credit cards.
>
> Pretty Woman

Financial geniuses summary

I found it pretty amazing that none of the financial advisers I interviewed left school wanting to become a career financial adviser. Most got there from a fairly different career path... from professional drumming, advertising and tourism to stockbrokers and bank clerks.

I loved learning that they all come from working class families and have invested in their technical skills and knowledge to help others learn from their wealth of knowledge.

What I also love is that nearly all of them also invest in their own constant personal and professional development, regardless of their current levels of success. There's always something new to be learned! What's at the top of your list?

There's a great lesson to be learned there. If elite athletes are still coached when at the top of their game, doesn't it make sense that the rest of us also commit to ongoing learning and growth?

The media would love to have us believe that the advice fraternity is full of wealthy fat cats leaching off poor unsuspecting citizens and sleazily separating them from their hard-earned wealth, when I've discovered hard working people who've fallen into a profession with the underlying desire to help their others succeed. And, from what I've seen, most of us don't need too much assistance in being parted from our earnings! And don't get me wrong, there's a few out there who aren't the nicest people and may fit that mould – but then sadly, you can find them anywhere, in all occupations and strata of society.

Another favourite of mine was don't take advice from broke people! So, no more hot stock tips from the taxi driver or your brother-in-law!

A strong theme was to understand your spending and take control of where your funds are going. Know your numbers! Don't live beyond your means came through loud and clear, but we'll only know if that's what we're doing if we've sat down and worked out what it costs us to live.

Making sure our protection strategies are in place was also vitally important. I'm very much an operator in the 'protect first' space. We've worked so hard for the things we have and as we know, life has a tendency to throw curve balls. Risk mitigation means we're better prepared to face the future when our Plan B is firmly established. If we don't have our ability to earn an income, our lifestyle and assets mean nothing, yet very few protect their income. Rather, they won't leave home without the car or home being protected. It's a really counter-intuitive approach and worth investigating.

> Formal education will make you a living;
> self-education will make you a fortune.
>
> Jim Rohn

Part III

Everyday heroes

Now, I've saved these guys until last because, truth be told, they may just be the ones you want to hear from the most.

Some of them are the battlers - those who go through their lovely lives every day, working for a living, making a home or a family or doing their very darnedest to make ends meet, keep the kids in uniforms, fund the school books and fees and get through to another pay period. For some people featured, their focus is on making a difference, and giving back over and above what they receive. It's about 'soul food' and investing in the greater good; but whatever their story, I've found them pretty inspirational.

You may not personally relate to the business gurus. Perhaps you've never had that stirring in the belly that drives you to take that great idea (I know you've had one!) and turn it into a reality. Seriously, as a teenager, I wanted a pony tail that went all the way down the back of my head and the next minute banana clips were invented! (Sorry if you missed the 1980s and have no idea what I'm talking about! Google them!) They were very cool and when I crimped my hair to wear in the clip, it was seriously amazing. My dad swears he thought up waterbeds before they got to market and my husband invented 24-hour gyms long before they were in Australia … none of which we patented or made a cent from. But I digress.

Perhaps the financial gurus don't do it for you either. Good for them, they know a thing or two about money. But maybe you feel they don't really connect with someone just like you. You've no interest really in taking your financial literacy to a whole new level, but feel you could totally learn a thing or two from some-one just like you.

You may be very happy with your lot in life, and that's a beautiful place to be. I actually hope you are. Those who know the magic of simplicity are truly blessed. Spending time with the poorest on Earth shows you how much unnecessary stuff we accumulate and what we truly can live without.

I hope you find some amazing people and stories here and that the lessons they share may be just what you're after.

Amy Neeson

Amy Neeson Photography

'It's just money; you can always make more.'

@AmyNeeson

Amy Neeson describes herself as a 'creative idealistic dreamer'. Born and raised on the Gold Coast, Australia, she grew up listening to INXS, writing poetry, drawing and wondering what wonderful things tomorrow would bring. At 19, she married her high-school sweetheart and now has two lovely children, a dog, and a great collection of vintage cameras.

Discovering a passion for photography at 17, she purchased her first film camera and started on a journey that would provide an amazing creative outlet and eventually an income to support herself and her family.

At 18, she completed a diploma in photojournalism, and immersed herself in learning as much as she could from books and magazines, prior to the age of digital cameras and the internet. Over time, Amy found herself travelling around Australia and internationally for weddings and photo shoots. She loves a challenge and a few years ago decided to add underwater photography to her style.

Now, with over 20 years' experience in the industry, Amy enjoys mentoring new photographers, sharing knowledge and teaching skills that she has learnt along the way. And she still has the same obsession with photography as she did all those years ago.

Okay, before you can get in and yell 'nepotism' at the top of your lungs, you need to know that Amy is my sister, so I've known her a while ... all her life, anyway! And if you're wondering why I'd put family in the book, please bear with me. Her story is definitely worth telling – even if you find yourself not quite believing it. And I kind of don't blame you; I've lived through it and it's still a little hard to comprehend.

I know there's a chance you're reading this thinking all those lessons from amazing businesspeople and financial professionals are great, but they don't apply to you. You're a battler, you work hard, don't seem to get ahead and things always go wrong; you barely make it from pay packet to pay packet. If that's you, I've thrown in this story especially for you.

Amy and I naturally grew up in the same home. I'm nearly three years older (although I rarely admit that and she stopped saying she was the eldest when I hit thirty-seven) and we have a younger brother. As I said earlier in my spiel, life was pretty middle class with local public primary schools and high schools within walking and bike-riding distance. I was definitely the fiercely protective, older sibling … even though it sometimes didn't do her much good.

University was never a goal for either of us, but we'd been encouraged to get a job or career that could set us up, pay the bills and keep life simple. Very early on, Amy chose a job in child care, but after constant bouts of sickness and increasing paper-work connected to auditing and keeping parents without custody away from those with, it all got a little hard. Amy went into retail sales for a while before reinventing herself as an amazing pho-tographer! (Yes, that is an unashamed plug!)

She married her high-school sweetheart, Mark, and it wasn't long before she was telling me that those maternal urges were calling. I must have looked at her pretty blankly because I'd fallen pregnant at 22 and had certainly never had a maternal calling, much less an urge, prior to that.

Their beautiful son, Billy, was born after a complicated birth and then, within three months, husband Mark was being airlifted by the CareFlight helicopter to the Prince Charles Hospital in Brisbane with a dissecting aortic aneurysm. He was 28 at the time. At that stage, they were renting a small two-bedroom fibro home in Palm Beach on the Gold Coast, where I'd also lived when I'd had my babies. And things got tough. Amy was no longer working because she had a new baby, and now Mark, who had been plastering since 16 and was the family breadwinner, was also out of action with the open-heart surgery. So this is where the 'have you had any financial setbacks?' part really starts.

A small insurance policy was found that provided around $300 per week income (although the providers did fight me that Mark may only be partially and not totally disabled for a time) and along with Centrelink (social security) payments, the generosity of friends and family helped get them through. I think over a dozen friends and family were in the waiting room to hear from the doctor when Mark came out of what was to be his first surgery.

We took turns at staying with him around the clock at the hospital because the drugs meant he was hallucinating and he'd go for a wander and not be able to find his way back to his room. When we couldn't find a place to stay close to the hospital, we were commuting daily over an hour each way. Eventually, Mark was discharged after three to four weeks in hospital.

Within three years, Amy came home to announce to Mark that she was expecting again, to which Mark advised that he now had another aneurysm where the valve attached to his heart had come away and he needed open heart surgery once again to repair the Dacron tubing to his aorta.

Amy's own heart had already been found to have arrhythmia, and she had flat-lined during a stress test and had fribulating arteries during an angiogram previously.

When their daughter, beautiful Tahlia, was born, she had an enlarged heart, four ventricular septal defects (holes in her heart), high blood pressure and cardiomyopathy; Mark had already had his second round of open heart surgery, and Billy was soon diagnosed as both severely autistic and intellectually impaired. Seriously…

But wait, there's more…

Mark has gone on to have a hernia repair and a melanoma removed from his arm. He's fallen through a scaffold and shattered his heel, needing twelve pins and a plate to fix it, and he then got staph in the wound meaning healing took an extra-long time. He has also had his optic nerve eaten out by the acanthamoeba parasite – a seriously nasty little beasty that invades the cornea … and we're just waiting for whatever comes next – and hoping and praying that it doesn't.

So, if you think you've battled financial and physical hardships, spare a thought for these guys.

For two years, they had to live in a caravan behind Mark's parent's home before finally becoming eligible for a lovely three-bedroom housing commission home that was just right to accommodate Billy's needs too.

I've possibly covered what family life was like growing up in my story but, as it turns out, we have different memories and versions of what did and didn't happen. The answers that follow cover some of her versions of events. But I'm the oldest, so mine is right.

What impact did your parents have on your financial abilities?

I don't think there was any direct bearing on my own abilities. I always thought that we were pretty destitute and didn't like asking for anything. I was sure we were poor. I actually hated living so frugally and would spend every penny that came my way. Even if I got 20 cents, I'd buy lollies as a treat.

We only shopped at thrift stores and Dad would put cardboard from cereal boxes in the bottom of our $6 canvas tennis shoes to make them last longer. I just knew that I never wanted to live that way.

What lessons did you learn from your parents about money?

My takeaway was that being frugal sucked. I thought it was an awful way to live and was determined to never set foot in a second-hand store again.

I later noticed the generosity of others and wanted to be more like them. I wanted to be in a position to help people and give back more.

My husband, Mark, would always buy quality items that would last for a long time rather than cheap items that fell apart, and that was very hard for me to adjust to after always having to look for bargains. It was incredibly rare for us to own anything new and buying off the rack was a once-in-a-lifetime treat!

I thought that money was very hard to come by and not to be wasted.

Do you stick to a family budget?

When we first got married, Mark was made redundant and we really had to take stock of our finances. I was working full-time and we had to make sure all the bills were paid first. After that, we had $5 left.

Growing up so frugally, although not ideal, was good practice for when this happened, as we were able to still make ends meet, if only just. We still make sure all our bills are covered first, but don't run a formal family budget.

We've never pooled our finances because we're both self-employed, but do have access to each other's accounts, so whoever has the money first, pays. It works for us.

What would you like Billy and Tahlia to learn about money?

Tahlia is a lot like me. She finds money and races to the nearest shopping centre to buy lollies. She is able to save though. She wanted to save $100 for spending money and purchase good quality clothing that she loved in her own style. She had to work by doing chores around the house to make the money. She had to pick up the dog poos, clean the mouse cage and help out with her brother, along with kitchen and household chores. She is also very generous. She recently bought packets of lollies and gave them all away to her friends. She gets mad at her stingy friends or if people aren't generous.

Every week, Billy has a school excursion where they walk to a local supermarket and purchase a drink, pay money and receive change. He can't do the counting, but he's understanding the principle of money. His kitchen jobs are to help unload the dishwasher and pack the cutlery away. He likes to vacuum too, whether it's plugged in or not!

I think we've covered your financial, emotional and physical setbacks; how did you recover?

We basically had to trade or work our way through. It feels like every time we pulled ourselves out of a hole, something else would happen. We're so grateful that our parents and in-laws did assist us financially, but mostly we've had to slog through when Mark was well enough to work and I had to keep working.

When Mark shattered his ankle, he had nine months off, so that was very difficult. After that, he'd work through the week when he could, and I'd do photography jobs on the weekend building my business, when he could mind the children.

What's the best financial advice you've ever been given?

My mother-in-law used to run the 'envelope system'. She had clear little plastic zipped envelopes with the name of each bill on them and would set aside funds each week so that when the bill came in, they were covered.

I've also learned you have to work hard to get ahead because of the number of setbacks we've constantly had. Mark was never a fan of insurances, but I wish we'd had some serious insurance in place that could have helped because we've only had little amounts that haven't really assisted us. Mark still struggles with his foot and walking and it's been nine years since the original injury. In a few years, he won't be able to work anymore and will become completely disabled from his injuries. He'll also likely become Billy's full-time carer when he finishes high school.

I also believe 'it's just money; you can always make more'.

How totally awesome is your financial adviser?

Pretty darn. It was great that we were able to fund some cover for me before I was diagnosed with the heart condition and that it could be paid for from our superannuation account. That's not ideal for everyone but it's really helped with our cash flow.

Mark had listened to many negative stories about insurance companies 'doing people over' and people not getting paid out and, consequently, hated insurance. It wasn't until we had a car written off and I found out that he'd let the insurance lapse that I then ensured we were covered for as much as we could be. Unfortunately, Mark's now uninsurable for obvious reasons and it's a bit late to try.

Looking back, it now makes sense to get insurance while you're healthy. Mark was super fit and would play tennis and football and go riding every week and no-one ever thought he'd have the health issues he now has, especially from such a young age.

Do you have a favourite form of investment?

Yes, but it's not financial; we don't have anything left over for that.

If anything, investing in my photography business has been a boon. It's a creative outlet for me and I've managed to travel around the world doing photo shoots. I love meeting other people and seeing how they live.

I like to learn new techniques and styles of photography. And I'm always scouting for interesting locations for my next shoot. Investing in experiences is paramount.

Key take-outs

Okay, so where do I even start with this one?

If you think you're 6 foot tall and bullet proof, think again. Things don't just happen to 'other people,' they can happen to you, and for some people, in spades.

I love Amy's tip to take out insurance while you're still healthy. It may seem counterintuitive, but when you see how things can go totally pear-shaped, you'll know that it's a great investment. On the flip side, I've also seen people cancel their insurances months before a serious diagnosis, so I always advise clients to get a complete medical prior to arranging insurance cancellations or reductions.

There are also occasions when all that great advice to pay yourself first just doesn't work. Paying the bills and eating must take priority in some situations over building up long-term savings, even if it's still a goal.

I also like the envelope system, although these days you no longer need physical envelopes. It's possible to BPAY or transfer funds each week for larger bills, or have various accounts where you can stash funds. Sometimes, it's even a great idea to set the money aside in your mortgage offset account to bring down interest on the home loan. However you do it, accounting for your bills, especially those big ones each pay period, is a great tip!

Also, living frugally may not be fun, but it can certainly teach some great lessons. With so many living beyond their means, being able to know just what's coming in and exactly where it has to go is a great skill. It also makes you a lot more creative about your forms of entertainment and dining out options. As some say, 'necessity is the mother of invention'.

Blessed are those who can give without
remembering, and take without forgetting.

Elizabeth Bibesco

Drew Gaffney

Professor of Medicine,
Vanderbilt University

'Money is necessary, but it's not
everything. It has a place as a
means but not as an "End".'

Francis Andrew 'Drew' Gaffney is an American doctor, professor of medicine at Vanderbilt University and previous employee of NASA – yes, he's a real-life astronaut, participating in the STS-40 Space Life Sciences (SLS 1) shuttle mission in 1991 as a payload specialist. According to his Wikipedia page (yes, he has one of those), 'The SLS-1 mission crew completed over 18 experiments in nine days, bringing back more medical data than any previous NASA flight.'

After graduating from high school in New Mexico, Drew completed a Bachelor of Arts degree from the University of California, Berkeley and then a Doctor of Medicine degree from the University of New Mexico, before serving as a flight surgeon at Ellington Air National Guard Base in Houston, Texas.

Drew next served as a visiting senior scientist with the Life Sciences Division at NASA Headquarters in the late 1980s, working with the Operational Medicine group and as Associate Manager of Biomedical Research as well as Program Scientist for the D-2 Spacelab mission and the Research Animal Holding Facility. He was a member of several working groups and implementation teams planning collaborative research with German, French and Soviet government scientists. He also served on a number of Space Station Freedom and advanced mission planning groups including the 'Humans to Mars' study group.

Drew's 15 years of experience in cardiac research and operation of equipment such as echocardiograms and rebreathing devices led to him being selected as a payload specialist aboard STS-40 Spacelab Life Sciences (SLS 1), a mission which took place in June 1991 and was the first Spacelab mission dedicated to biomedical studies. He was a co-investigator on an experiment that studied human cardiovascular adaption to space flight.

Following this flight, Dr Gaffney became a member of the Institute of Medicine's Committee on Space Biology and Medicine, serving from 1992 to 2000. He is a professor of medicine (cardiovascular disease) at Vanderbilt University and continues to serve as a consultant and reviewer for human *spaceflight-related studies, with over 50 publications in the areas of cardiovascular regulation and space physiology.*

Drew is the only person I've interviewed who I haven't actually met 'in the flesh'... yet!

When I was chatting with Maree Lallensack, the regional manager of my licensee, about my book project and told her I was interviewing some wonderful everyday heroes, she said, 'How about interviewing an astronaut?' Naturally, my ears pricked up and I wanted in! Maree has sailed around the world and met some amazing people on her travels. Drew and his lovely wife, Lili, happen to be just two of them. Perhaps our paths will cross sometime in the future on my travels to the United States, if the planets align. Drew and Lili still enjoy sailing and spending time with their extended family, children and grandchildren.

I'd like to understand a little about your background. What was family life like when you were growing up?

I was born and raised in a small desert town in New Mexico, the eldest of five sons, born over 13 years. My family had a strong work ethic and highly valued education. Neither of my parents completed university; first World War II (WWII) intervened, then family. We lived in a home that my father and his father built just after the war. I attended parochial school *[a church school]* through to grade 8, and then public school. Boy Scouts was important, as were various school activities.

My parents supported us all through five bachelor of arts (BA) degrees, two masters of science (MS) and one doctor of medicine (MD).

Our town integrated its schools in 1954 following the Brown v. Board of Education of Topeka Supreme Court decision, in which the Court declared state laws establishing separate public schools for black and white students to be unconstitutional. That decision disallowed the 'separate but equal' doctrine. Ours was one of a few in New Mexico that integrated and this had a big impact on the students there and the value of diversity. My maternal grandfather was a New Mexico native and taught me Spanish as child, which has come in very useful over the rest of my life. When I graduated from high school, I'd travelled about 450 miles from the town in which I was raised. College was almost 2000 miles away. From there, I went all over the world, travelling, working and living.

After graduating from high school, I went to UC Berkeley, PreMed, and then UNM medical school. I completed a residency in internal medicine, a fellowship in cardiology, and then became professor of medicine, active physician and scientist for the next 45 years.

Where did you learn about money?

My family did not have money. My father, after leaving the military following WWII, became a potash miner and then bank teller, and my mother was a secretary at local mining company.

My parents worked very hard to support their large family. All five sons worked from an early age, not to support the family, but to be able to buy the things the family couldn't provide for us. The lessons I learned were more about the value of work, education and also honesty.

What impact did your family have on your financial abilities?

The value of money as a tool was very clear. One got money by working hard, and working honestly. That was the rule, but there was no pressure or drama with it. The general rule was that hard work and high performance were generally - albeit, not always - rewarded. We all learned to save for things we wanted and set long-term goals. We also learned to save and invest. I owned stock that I bought from my own savings when I was 12 years old.

My father worked his way up from bank teller to bank president. It took him about 20 years to do so. In his 60s, the bank he ran was bought by a holding company that engaged in highly dishonest activities. My father was fired for opposing their schemes. The bank went bankrupt and my father lost much of his life's savings. He worked into his 70s to be sure our mother was financially secure. Family members were very helpful, as were people whom he'd helped over the years. Many people came to his funeral (at age 85) to tell stories of how he'd helped them when they were just starting their first job, when they'd gotten into financial difficulty, and so on. I knew many of them, but did not know about what my father had done for them.

'If it seems too good to be true, it probably is' from my father. Work hard, never waste money, save for a rainy day, and never be greedy. Trying to find 'win–win' solutions is always better than making a killing at someone else's expense. All from my father. I guess this is why he'd never be president of the US …

Don't buy stocks in individual companies. Stick with index and exchange-traded funds.

Money is necessary, but it's not everything. It has a place as a means but not as an 'End'. My children have worked hard, got their educations, and are now professionals. Money is a means, not an end.

Do you have a personal or family budget? Do you stick to it? Does it guide your spending?

We have an approximate budget, but spend more by what we need or want, for what, and its value to us. It makes no sense to buy things just because there's money to do so. Likewise, if something's really important, it's often possible to find a way to obtain it. 'Value' is very important - that is, to take care of one's family first, educate one's children, plan for 'old age' and leave something for one's children. We know how much we need in the various categories, but it's not as proactive as it is a monitoring function. There's often a lot of leeway in the price of what one wants.

If you have a business, how important is annual forecasting and budgeting?

Absolutely necessary. Profit is one of the goals of most businesses. It's hard to make a profit without forecasting and budgeting.

Do you use or have you ever used a financial adviser? Do you see a benefit in dealing with a finance professional?

I engaged my first financial advisor when I became a physician, was beginning to have a good salary, and was convinced by colleagues that I 'had' to have an advisor. I wasn't terribly happy with the advisor's suggestions, but went along. My losses were almost a full year's salary. He'd put my money into an enormous real estate fraud. It was a valuable lesson, especially on how to assess advisors, if nothing else.

I still do use financial advisors and I have my investments distributed between two major firms. All the investments are index or exchange based and I use a 50-50 split between equity and fixed-income assets. Even though the market has gone crazy, I've stuck with rebalancing.

I had most of my money with a different firm but pulled it all when I realised that they were not a fiduciary relationship. It became obvious that their goal was to 'sell products' and not help their clients manage their accounts.

What's your favourite form of investment?

Index funds. My favourite 'gurus' are David Swenson from Yale University and Warren Buffett. The only stock I own is in Berkshire Hathaway *[of which Buffett is Chief Executive Officer and Chairman]*. Everything else is in index funds.

My key take-outs

Drew comes from a modest background, yet from a generation that still highly values education. Today, college dropouts can become successful entrepreneurs and billionaires and a formal education seems to be less valued. Yet, if you don't have that next bright idea or the drive to set up a multinational company, formal education can still provide fabulous opportunities to not only makes ends meet, but also provide a comfortable lifestyle and retirement … let alone being able to head into space!

I also liked Drew's point to be careful in your choice of professionals. If something doesn't feel right in your gut, you should question what you've been recommended and why. Advisers need to provide advice that is in your best interests and will still allow you to sleep at night.

Saving for the things you want and setting long-term goals is also a great tip and, although not new, something that many still know, but don't do. Is there just one goal you can set today and start working towards?

Drew's father sounds like a practical man with much common sense. Creating situations that are win–win instead of gaining advantage at others' expense is a fabulous sentiment. Drew's also developed a technique that works for him and suits how he likes to invest. Again, it's great to understand what you're investing in and, when you find something you're comfortable with and understand, stick with it. And if you aren't sure what to do, check out the gurus who have been super successful and walk their own talk.

> My favourite things in life don't cost any money.
>
> Steve Jobs

Ann-Marie Von Douglas

Vocal coach and civil celebrant

'I believe in keeping it simple and ensuring my monthly outgoings are covered.'

Ann-Marie Von Douglas grew up in Sydney in a theatrical family. She studied at the Sydney Conservatorium of Music (voice and piano) after leaving school, working in theatres and movie theatres at night to pay her fees along with singing in pubs and clubs around Sydney. Ann-Marie also did voice overs for radio station 2KY and performed in various stage productions such as Oklahoma and Fiddler on the Roof.

Ann-Marie then went flying as an air hostess for three years, before marrying and having to retire, as was the law back then. She then lived in Europe, also working occasionally in clubs.

On her return to Australia and Sydney in the 1970s, she divided her time between raising her two daughters, running a lunch bar in Willoughby and working with her daughters' school in music and theatre production. She moved to the Gold Coast in 1990, where she worked a few seasons with Gold Coast Little Theatre, playing in The Sound of Music, Auntie Mame and several one-act plays.

Ann-Marie is now working as a vocal coach with private students in her home and with students at a local Performance Academy, and is also a civil celebrant, happily marrying lovely couples, doing vow renewals and naming babies – able to conduct ceremonies in English and German – which she says is great fun and something she loves. She has two married daughters and two grandchildren.

After starting work for radio station 94.1 in late 2004, Ann-Marie took six months off to return to Europe in 2005 before returning to the airwaves in 2006. Sadly, she needed to take six months off work because of breast cancer in 2010, but returned to radio again in 2011. She is now a happy advocate for fundraising events for this horrible disease, along with also being an advocate for Asperger's syndrome and autism, because she has a daughter and a grandson with this disorder.

Okay, now it's time for me to let the cat out of the bag. Lovely Annie happens to be my singing teacher … and no, I'm not any good, I just love belting out a tune – badly or otherwise – in the shower or in the car. And this is the poor lady who has to listen to my warbling and try to turn it into something that won't make her ears bleed on a weekly basis or, at best, something resembling a tune. She patiently sets exercises, has me work through them and provides the music for me to sing along to - mostly in the car or shower. And no, you'll never find me on TV shows like X Factor or [Somewhere's] Got Talent.

As you may have gathered, Annie also happens to be crazy talented herself and still continues part-time work. Having lived and worked all over the world, she believes the Gold Coast is the place she's now meant to be. Her answers to my questions provide more details.

I'd like to understand a little about your background. What was family life like when you were growing up?

I grew up in an extended family with my parents, grandmother, a spinster aunt and my older twin brothers. My parents were apart for around six years during World War II because my father worked in Papua New Guinea as an Adjutant to the Air Vice Marshall and then worked on the war crimes tribunal also. He was shot down during the war and returned for R&R in 1944, and the twins soon followed. He returned home again in 1946 after the war, and I turned up in 1947.

My mother was the youngest of 13 children and it was her mother and sister who also stayed with us while my father was away. Mum took in 'piecework' and sewed boot tops to help cover the private high school fees for the three of us.

When Dad returned, he ran movie theatres. He was told that he wasn't cutthroat or ruthless enough to be a business man.

I studied at the Sydney Conservatorium of Music and worked in theatres to cover my fees. I'd been in a three-year relationship with a policeman who was 10 years older than me, but grew out of him. I then became a private airline hostess during the 'jet set' era, which was pretty glamourous. When I was 22, however, I met an incredibly handsome German Count, who completely swept me off my feet. We met on 3 March and were married on 30 May. It was a bit of a whirlwind!

From 1971 to 1974 we lived in Germany, where I learned to speak the language. My husband's father ran car dealerships and we'd drive luxury vehicles to drop them off when they needed delivering and found our way to St. Moritz, Corsica and all over Europe. My father-in-law was an associate of General Tito [then president of Yugoslavia] and thought himself a bit of a ladies' man who'd holiday with different young women, visiting hunting lodges and various countries very regularly.

The family were related to the original Scottish Black Douglas family, and his father was the head of the European clan of Von Douglas and had a castle in Europe. Sadly, he was wastrel, interested mostly in money and sex and both wasted his own inheritance and stole the inheritance from his sons, who were supposed to inherit the first spring water business that had been established.

We had a very lavish lifestyle, prestige cars, travel, boats and more.

It wasn't until we moved back to Australia and had our daughters in 1975 and 1977 that things went a bit pear-shaped. My husband ran luxury car dealerships too and was a talented valuer, but eventually became an alcoholic and ended up being sacked from a few jobs and finally left after 32 years of marriage.

Where did you learn about money?

I've never learned about money. My husband took care of everything once I'd left paid employment because 'the Douglas wives didn't work'.

I'd followed some tips of my father's when I was working as a private air hostess but, apart from that, have never really learned what to do or how it works.

Separating from my husband was a massive setback. He'd siphoned off everything we'd owned over some months to start over with a new partner and all I was left with was $70,000 in the bank before I found out.

I don't think I've ever recovered from that. I've had to nurse that little nest egg to keep me going since that time. I also needed to reinvent myself and get back into the workforce with the skills I hadn't used since before I'd gotten married.

I have a daughter and grandson with special needs and my other daughter had legal battles and I try to help them financially when I can.

My father gave me a great tip and I'm not sure where he got it from, because he was an orphan. He had always told me to keep one-third of my take-home wage in an emergency fund, then pay my rent and health insurance and I'd get to live on the rest.

I still do that now.

I'd pass on what my father told me. It's worked for me, and since my marriage breakdown, I've adopted the strategy once again, especially now that I'm on the age pension with only a little cash in the bank to tide me over.

I've passed on what my father told me but, hey, they're my kids. They don't listen to me!

Do you have a personal budget? Do you stick to it? Does it guide your spending?

Yes, I still keep funds aside from my pension, and then make sure my rent and health insurance are paid followed by my general living expenses like phone and utilities. I have to be careful now that I have to rely on the pension. My singing students and wedding services provide that little bit extra for the occasional luxury.

Do you use or have you ever used a financial adviser? Do you see a benefit in dealing with a finance professional?

Looking back, I wish we had. I just figured that my husband knew what he was doing and had it all covered. I don't think I ever questioned what went on in the business. I just had to sign and that was very typical of wives during that time period.

And these days, no. I have used a tax agent recently and that was great because I was able to save on what I'd been charged and maximise my tax refunds.

What's your favourite form of investment?

These days, I can't afford to take a risk so cash and term deposits are my preferred investments. I'm not greedy and don't need a lot. I believe in keeping it simple and need to ensure my monthly outgoings are covered, preferably by the interest on my investments.

Having said that, I also love investing in creativity. I love writing and delivering beautiful wedding ceremonies. The DJ work I did also was a creative outlet. And I enjoy nurturing my spirituality. There's so much to invest in!

Key take-outs

I love Annie's tip to keep it simple. She's certainly lived an amazing life during the 'jet set' era, saw some amazing places and totally 'lived it up'!

To go from that crazy, international jet-setting lifestyle to now being a pensioner is a complete turnaround, yet she manages beautifully with her simple philosophy. Moving from the 'champagne lifestyle' to a 'beer budget' isn't easy for many to transition to, but sometimes 'needs must' and Annie is the perfect example that it can be done – although it sure takes attention to detail.

The idea of setting aside a percentage of wages for long-term savings is pervasive, so I guess there's something to that. Whether it's 15 per cent or 30 per cent, setting aside something for the long term is vitally important and a top tip from quite a few of those interviewed. I'd love to know how much you think is practical.

It's also very interesting to note that Annie really didn't know what was going on in the family business, as was once the general pattern for many wives. Hopefully now, if you're a signatory on a business, you take a much more active interest in what's happening and what you're signing your name to.

> If you want to know what God thinks of money,
> just look at the people he gave it to.
>
> Dorothy Parker

Peter Baines, OAM

Global speaker, charity founder, consultant and author

'Work hard, invest, take advice but, above all of that, make the time and space to enjoy what you're creating around your wealth.'

@peter_baines
@HATWAustralia

Peter Baines tells it like it is. He doesn't come from academia and he doesn't theorise on what makes good leaders; what he does do is share stories from some of the largest disaster and crisis scenes we have experienced in our lifetime.

Peter was on the ground, leading teams in Bali after the 2002 bombings, he was one of the international leaders who spent several months in Thailand after the Boxing Day tsunami and he was also sent to Saudi Arabia and Japan after disasters hit both of those countries. During this time, he was leading both the Australian and international teams in the multi-jurisdictional responses. His performance in these areas saw him seconded to work for Interpol in Lyon, France, leading a counterterrorism project for the member countries of Interpol, focusing on chemical, biological, radiological and nuclear threats and trends. Completing his time with Interpol, he then spent time advising the United Nations Office on Drug and Crime in South-East Asia on leadership and counterterrorism.

Leaving that behind, he went on to build international aid agency Hands Across the Water, which at the time of writing is on track to pass the $20 million mark since he established it in 2005. This, along with sharing powerful keynote presentations across the globe, is where he spends his time now. In January 2014, Peter Baines was recognised in the Australia Day honours with the awarding of the Order of Australia Medal for his international humanitarian work, and in 2016 he received the Most Admirable Order of Direkgunabhorn, awarded by the King of Thailand for his devotional services to the Kingdom of Thailand.

I first had the privilege of hearing Peter speak as a keynote at a financial planning conference I attended in 2008. Peter shared his story of moving from forensic police work, which he'd been assigned to do in Thailand after the Boxing Day Tsunami in 2004, and how he'd come to start the charity Hands Across the Water (HATW), which supports disadvantaged children in Thailand. I can tell you that there weren't too many dry eyes in the house by the end of his presentation.

I had a few friends after that time became very involved with the work of HATW. These friends loved returning annually to take part in the fundraising bike rides – some cycling 800 kilometres and even 1600 kilometres, raising over $10,000 each leg, to participate in the events that finish at the orphanages that the funds support and be welcomed into the arms and smiles of the children.

In 2016, I was pleased to support the annual Future of Leadership Forum, where all proceeds go to the HATW charity. First-class speakers donate their time and fund their way to the event, with hundreds of thousands of dollars being raised that all goes back to the children. And I mean 100 per cent!

At that event, a raffle was held with the one lucky winner taking part in the new Social Venture Program that Soulful Experiences had arranged in partnership with Hands Across the Water – and yours truly scored the win! I can't begin to tell you how excited I was to win a trip to the Bangkok slums and the orphanages in Northern Thailand – I guess it's not a prize that everyone would love, but it sure was a treat for me and another life-changing experience. I truly felt like I'd won Willy Wonka's Golden Ticket!

A group of around a dozen of us assisted in the demolition of a home (not a home by our standards) in the Khlong Toei slums so that local builders could build a new, sturdy home for an amazingly deserving family. (You can find out more about this adventure in my blog at www.financechicks.com.) We then headed north to assist two orphanages, Home Hug 1 and 2, with projects that needed completing. We collaborated with the children and each other on a design for a mural to decorate an outside wall at the first orphanage to make the home more welcoming to outsiders. We also helped pave an entrance and spread a gravel driveway to assist at Home Hug 2. The children kept us well supplied with cool towels for our necks in the heat and searing Thai humidity, and plied us with snacks, ice-creams *and food throughout the day, along with fabulous dancing and entertainment with our evening meal.*

We were able to meet Mae Thiew, the 'mother' who has dedicated her life to caring for the children and, aside from being a monk, would have to possibly be the closest thing to a real-life saint you could ever meet. Her dedication and devotion to the children is second to none and it was among many tears and hugs and waves and cheering that we departed when our jobs were done. Sharing in school pick up was a real treat and even being allowed to follow Mae Thiew as she collected donations from the local community was an amazing experience. Her own health battles never diminish her smiles and efforts.

Peter speaks across three main areas – leadership, engagement and profitable corporate social responsibility platforms – within his Leadership Matters, Experience Matters and Doing Good by Doing Good presentations. Peter works with each of his clients to tailor the presentation to fit the brief for that particular audience.

His answers to my questions provide more detail in some of these areas, and you can also catch Peter via @peter_baines and @HATWAustralia.

I'd like to understand a little about your background. What was family life like when you were growing up?

I grew up in the western suburbs of Sydney. Mum and Dad separated when I was around 12. I was the middle child, with an older brother and younger sister. We lived in Georges Hall and I was there until I was around 19, when I moved out and lived with mates.

There was never too much money around. Dad was a Commonwealth driver for politicians, working long hours, and his overtime paid the bills. We didn't see him often at night and he worked weekends too. We had a very working-class background. There were never any overseas trips until I could pay my own way. Family holidays were spent just a few hours out of Sydney, and we did sport on weekends.

After high school, I went to Wollongong University and enrolled in an arts degree, but even now am not sure why. Six months later, I didn't know why I was there and so left and got a job at Grace Brothers. Then I decided to join the police service, enrolled, was selected and sworn in.

I'd left school in 1984 and by July 1986 was in the police force. I was in uniform for four and a half years. My first assignment was in Merrylands but it was a bit of a retirement village back then, very quiet and pretty boring. I put in for a transfer to Cabramatta, which was much busier; we had work to do there and I enjoyed the busyness.

But it wasn't long until I was sick of dealing with drunks and domestics. I was called out to help people who'd been married longer than I'd been alive, to sort out their marital woes. Friday nights saw the drunks spill out of the Diggers Club and want to use the station toilets or use the phone to call taxis.

I then applied for the forensic services group and moved into the Sydney CBD for 18 months, and then to a country posting in Tamworth. Back then, Tamworth had a population of around 30,000 and I loved living rural. I was happy to go bush, and ended up getting married and staying in country New South Wales from 1992 to 2001. I studied science and did my law degree while there. I went as constable, then become a sergeant in crime scene investigations, then made Detective Inspector and moved back to Sydney with the family, which now included children, at the end of 2001.

Where did you learn about money?

I had no formal lessons around money; no mentors advised me on wealth creation, retention or how to be fiscally responsible. I grew up to be tight with money because it was so hard to come by and there was so little. I was always cautious with spending. I had a greater appreciation for money after my parents' separation – we really scraped and learned to enjoy what we had.

Obviously, the salary is set in the police force, so the income is set. Overtime is the only bonus – you can't work harder and earn more. It's pretty hard to pick up another shift. Only a disaster while you were on call would mean any extra money. You need to learn to live within your means when on a salary. It's all you get.

At 18, I bought a block of land with my girlfriend (later wife). We both got a personal loan for $10,000 each and purchased land on the Sunshine Coast in Queensland. I'm not sure where the motivation for that came from, as my family never had done that. But it was something I wanted to do, rather than spend on cars or waste funds. It was something we could hold on to. Before we married, we also bought an investment property in Dolls Point, southern Sydney.

When we moved, we kept properties and rented in Tamworth, but soon worked out that it was cheaper to buy a small place and renovate. We also bought units in Tamworth as an investment. I got interested in property and understanding negative and neutral gearing and positive growth properties. We always knew what we could do on a fixed income. The properties needed to be positively geared and paying their own way from the start. We just didn't have money to spend on them to cover interest or maintenance. At one stage, we had six units, plus our house, land and investment properties. If I learned, it was by doing.

Once you're set up, get divorced and start again. That's the best way to have a financial setback! My wife and I separated in 2005 once we were back in Sydney. It was the toughest time ever for me, both financially and emotionally. I'd been working overseas after the Boxing Day Tsunami and we separated between tours. I was living on a couch with friends. When back in Thailand, I decided I needed a place to stay and, after my third tour, had nowhere to go. I had the bag I'd packed to head overseas with and an unmarked police car. I moved into some very dodgy places, and every few nights a new boarding house. All my worldly belongings were in the car. I had no money. I worked out the bills that needed to be paid to support the family. My wife was working part-time. I worked out what it'd cost for my family to keep the same lifestyle. I rented in a home in Castle Hill and had $80 left per fortnight to live. I couldn't afford a personal car, and I ate very lean and lived in an incredibly sparse house.

It was around this time I was asked by a friend I'd worked with in Thailand if I would be up to some fundraising to help the kids we'd seen over there who'd been orphaned after the disaster. I was at the lowest point in my life and going through my divorce. It's at this time friends are choosing sides and my life was turned upside down. Holding fundraising dinners was definitely not on the radar.

Committing to raise funds for kids in Thailand to have a home when I didn't have one myself was a juxtaposition, but I said yes and started public speaking. I had been asked to share my story and be paid for it! Originally, I thought it was a dumb idea and threw away the business card of the person who'd suggested it. I didn't know what I could possibly have to offer large corporate groups. But then I thought, *What if it was true and I worked on a keynote?* I decided to call him and learn more and see if maybe I could make some money.

So, I did. I went on the speaking tour and was paid for my story. As it worked out, I raised money for the home for the kids in Thailand and my speaking business grew. Financial recovery started right then.

I eventually had to resign from the police force. I'd worked in France, for Interpol, the United Nations, Saudi Arabia, Japan – and more opportunities kept coming for the speaking. It just grew, and Hands Across the Water grew – so I had to make a decision about where I put my time. I was still on secondment from the NSW police force, and this was supposed to be for one year but was extended. I was working in counterterrorism and watching the growth of HATW. Money was coming in, and I had to make a choice – to stop speaking, which meant no more money for HATW and the kids, or quit the normal job. A normal job means no flexibility – I requested 12 months' leave without pay to focus on the charity but that was denied, so I resigned.

I set up Peter Baines Consulting and starting doing many more speaking engagements and running leadership programs. Good income was coming in for HATW and things were getting better for the charity and for me. I wanted to finalise my property settlement, and looked at selling the units we had in Tamworth. I was still paying child support, the family home mortgage and bills. All these commitments ended up feeling like a noose around my neck and I needed it dealt with and finalised. I got good financial advice and learned that I could borrow against our assets. I finally bought my ex-wife out of her share, and she lived in the home rent-free with the children. I felt like I was in a much better position.

When I'd originally bought properties in Tamworth, I'd spoken with my accountant. I remember them telling me, 'Once you've settled, it'll come back and reward you, and you'll be in a good position someday.' And it was true.

Later, I remarried and my new wife and I bought in Nar-rabeen. We renovated and rebuilt basically due to proceeds from the sale of the units in Tamworth. I also sold a property in

Castle Hill and have now bought a 100-acre farm as well. It was absolutely a love purchase and a lifestyle decision. I can't tell you how much I feel a connection to that land and want it to stay in use for the family. I can't imagine ever parting with this property – and I'm not someone who usually gets emotionally attached to real estate. I still have my home on the beach and now the farm! I feel incredibly blessed from a financial point of view. My main motivator was to share the farm with family and friends, to have a place to share with our kids and extended families. We'll never rent it out; it's a place to create memories and experiences. If I hadn't been working and speaking, I wouldn't have been able to get the first mortgage to get the Castle Hill property, which provided the capital growth to allow me to buy the farm.

I guess I've been able to generate wealth not really knowing what I was doing. How lucky am I? I've also been able to assist the kids in Thailand to have a home, food and medication.

For me, it's never been about amassing money in the bank. Buying the farm has helped me with a big mindset shift. I am so grateful. Whenever I'm there, I think, *Look at what we've got; we're so lucky*, and I thoroughly enjoy it.

I look back now at that really hard time in 2005 and 2006 and see how everything has turned around for me. I put it all back to saying yes to helping the kids in Thailand. Without that decision, at my lowest point, I wouldn't have started public speaking, which led to consulting, and now assisting in building corporate responsibility programs and so much more.

What's the best financial advice you've ever been given, and who was it from?

I thought that getting a good solid job was the best advice ever, and the police offered great health care and benefits. I was a part of the First State Super plan pre-1988; a scheme that almost sent the NSW state government broke. You were guaranteed a pension for life. But when I resigned at the end of 2008, I left all those benefits behind. I had been there 22 years, was a Detective Inspector and had won lots of awards. But only when I checked my bank balance one day and saw that it had gone up by $50,000, did I know that part of my life was over. There was no separation certificate or notice, just a termination transaction into my bank account.

Not long after, I went to a doctor for a lump on my leg. I was told that I had malignant melanoma. I had a biopsy, scored 20 stitches and was told that they'd got it. So off I went speaking again. I was in Perth when I got an urgent call from the doctor, telling me to go to hospital that day, the cancer was back. I really couldn't because I was away, so I finished my two speaking gigs, flew home and walked into surgery. I was told I now had an aggressive tumour, was referred to the oncology unit at Royal Prince Alfred Hospital and the next moment was talking survival rates with a professor. Somehow, everything had seemed to escalate very quickly. And I had no health cover, life insurance or benefits. In the weeks between walking away and letting every-thing go, I was now talking about my life expectancy. Thankfully, I'm alive to tell the tale.

I met a financial adviser who had seen me speak in 2007, and he contacted me after the conference, wanting to help raise funds for HATW. At this stage, I had some superannuation savings but nothing else. Lee Virgin went on to become my friend and my adviser. He went into bat for me and got me some limited insurance cover, naturally excluding cancer, and then, later, full cover. I put all my financial affairs in his hands. I'm the first to admit when I don't know something and, when it came to insurance and retirement savings, I knew nothing. Income insurance was not something I knew about. I just laid it before Lee and he helped me structure it.

Since then, I've engaged accountants and set up proper structures, like companies and trusts. I'm a firm believer in surrounding yourself with people who know what you don't.

I look at the position I'm in now and I'm so grateful. Work hard, invest, take advice but, above all of that, make the time and space to enjoy what you're creating around your wealth. I love the farm and feel it's probably the best decision I've made – maybe not the smartest or best financially, but best for the serenity and the lifestyle.

Just ask yourself, at what point do you say, 'Now I'll enjoy it'?

As a legacy for your children, what would you like them to learn about money?

I talk to my kids about their ability to get into the local property market. Sydney prices are scary now, but I've also told them not to be afraid to buy into more rural places – preferably positively or neutrally geared. You don't need lots of money to start a financial investment strategy.

I know property and it's been kind to me. It feels relatively safe, and has provided good long-term growth. Turn your attention to that early.

Do you have a personal or family budget? Do you stick to it? Does it guide your spending?

Yes, I remarried a few years ago and my wife, Claire (aka CT), and I run a budget and review it regularly. CT had her own place in Ryde and we lived together for a while before buying the place together in Narrabeen. There's been constant change in our lives – a major renovation, the farm purchase, and regular travel to Thailand and New Zealand. We also review finances every time there's a big change.

We now have shared financial goals and shared budgeting, and understand how to meet our regular expenses. We're both self-employed, which means nothing is certain about when and how much we're getting in. She's still starting out and growing her business.

Do you use or have you ever used a financial adviser? Do you see a benefit in dealing with a finance professional?

We've just seen a planner together for the first time to discuss our shared goals. I see the benefits as knowing the best thing to do, understanding tax minimisation strategies, setting a plan for wealth creation, and looking at levels of insurance cover in event of injury, illness or death. We're able to establish structures to meet our dreams and wishes, both now and even post death, and have these set in place.

What's your favourite form of investment?

Property has been safe, advantageous and relatively easy for me to understand. I'm a simple person, and try to invest wisely. My retirement savings are managed by a planner and are exposed to the share market but it's not something I'm very familiar with.

Investing in your own happiness brings a lot of returns. Shared experiences and supporting others are the best investments. Even my current prosperity can be traced back to that decision to do the home for kids in Thailand, and I can tell you that I've benefited 100 times more than my contributions to Thailand.

My key take-outs

I love how Peter's current journey all seems to have started from that decision to help others. He was certainly at rock bottom and could hardly have been blamed if he'd said no and that he needed to sort his own personal situation out first. But it's often only by looking back that we get to see those pivot points in our lives.

I know that children in Thailand have benefited greatly from the work Peter has done there, and it's been a privilege to have a very small role in that – and I can't wait for more.

Peter also was content to 'stick to his knitting'. He knew property and understood how it worked. He made sure that he wasn't making reckless decisions and getting in over his head. The properties had to meet the criteria he'd set of being neutrally or positively geared and he was happy to take a very long-term position.

Sometimes, understanding one thing very well may be a more effective strategy than trying lots of different things that we don't really understand, and not doing any of them very well.

> If we do nothing, nothing will ever change.
>
> Peter Baines, OAM

Everyday heroes summary

So how great were some of these stories? We heard from people who'd walked away from corporate lives to start a charity or even now rely on the support of the social security system to help their families make ends meet! Talk about heroes!

I also get the very solid learning that our success is completely unrelated to our level of resources, but is totally about our resourcefulness. It's what you do with what you've got that makes all the difference!

I'm sure we've all met people on average incomes whose homes are full of 'stuff' – which is precisely what they have to show for all their earnings. Maybe it would fetch a few thousand dollars at a car boot sale! Then there's those quiet achievers we come across who don't earn much differently, but who we're surprised to learn have a little share portfolio building away or even an investment property or two.

I also love the ability of these heroes to live within their means. It's a lesson that many advisers try to constantly impart to their clients, but with the ready availability of credit and the rise of payWave and Paypass and the cashless society, it seems to be much easier said than done.

Understanding exactly what is coming in and, more importantly, going out is imperative. And although it's fabulous to be able to live on just part of our wage as an ideal, that doesn't always work for everyone. Knowing your numbers is vital to being able to make ends meet.

Also, get insurance while you're still fit and healthy! Although it makes sense in theory, not everyone does it and you can end up with expensive loadings or exclusions on your policies once pre-existing conditions have been diagnosed – or, even worse, you become uninsurable.

> A budget is telling your money where to go
> instead of wondering where it went.
>
> Dave Ramsey

Findings

So how completely fascinating was that? I totally loved getting to know each of these people better and hearing their stories. It was a total privilege to have those interviewed let me in on their early family lives and secrets, and hear the lessons that were passed on during childhood, whether spoken or unspoken. And, truly, not everyone wanted to be so revealing. Hard to believe but, despite my charm and charisma, I was turned down by some.

Through the interviews, a fairly common theme seemed to emerge of a more conservative parents' or grandparents' generation, which makes perfect sense, based on their circumstances. Those of our ancestors who lived through war, a stock market crash, the Great Depression and more wars know what it's like to go without. They know about making things last and getting the final bit of use out of whatever item is available. They know from very personal experience that good times are followed by bad, and that being conservative means we won't lose as much as others who are exposed to more risky styles of investment.

There's no denying, however, that today's millennials (including gen Y and those born between 1977 and 1995), and beyond, greatly differ from previous generations in many ways. This isn't surprising when you think about the very different world they've grown up in – the internet was (nearly) always there, rapid computing advancements have happened for their entire lives, they've been joined at the hip to their phones since high school and major financial events such as the global financial crisis (GFC) have come and gone without leaving a blip on their radar, to name just a few. These experiences have led to some quite different and easily discernible behavioural and attitudinal differences from the previous generations like gen X and the baby boomers. We've also now lived in the longest period of 'peace' in an incredibly long time – I'm talking a simplistic version of world peace here, not including countries at war and large skirmishes and Middle Eastern conflict, although I'm sure many will wish to correct me. All this basically means is that for a couple of generations, good times have not been followed by bad on a global scale.

There always certain areas, however, where all our needs are quite similar, and that's true of our finances. Just like the generations before them, millennials along with the rest of us need to save for their future, manage their debt levels and ensure they protect their assets and loved ones. The financial challenges they face may not be exactly the same as those that have gone before, but the need for objective and professional advice is. They too need to address the lessons that their parents have passed down as their legacy.

It looks like there's been a lot of childhood lessons around money – some taught, others unspoken but still passed on – that, in turn, become our beliefs, limiting or otherwise, around money.

Some of these lessons might be:

- money doesn't grow on trees
- it takes money to make money
- money is the root of all evil
- love of money is the root of evil
- the rich get richer, the poor get poorer
- you have to work really hard to get ahead
- I'm just no good with money
- we've never been a rich family
- money is a limited resource
- wanting more money is greedy or selfish
- a good education is vital to getting a good job and success
- only those prepared to break the law will ever get ahead
- I'll never get ahead
- I could never handle money anyway
- I just wouldn't know what to do with it
- I'll never have enough to share or give away
- if I have more than enough, then someone else is missing out
- I hate money/thinking about money/dealing with money/ talking about money
- take care of the pennies and the pounds take care of themselves.

You get the point… and the list goes on and on. Some of these you may still totally believe, and I know there's at least one there that I do! So, what to do about it?

Maybe, first, tick those that resonate with you. What thoughts or ideas do you most identify with from the list? What ones have you heard or actually believe? Have you said those things to yourself or your children?

I know I'm totally guilty of having thought, truly believed or said some of those beliefs myself in the past. What, then, are the alternate options? What could you replace those beliefs with to try to tap into the 'abundance mindset' that a few interviewees mentioned?

I'm certainly no guru or hold a psychology degree. And I can't say that I'm super comfortable reciting affirmations over my cornflakes or avocado on toast for breakfast, but I'm assured that some of these positive beliefs are a brilliant alternate to those mentioned previously. (Trust me, I'm a financial adviser!) I'm even told that you don't need to believe them to start with! So, why not try some of these on for size:

- I feel richer every day.

- I love money and money loves me.

- I attract money.

- I am receiving money now.

- I have more than enough money.

- I am willing, ready and able to receive money.

- I see abundance everywhere.

- I am a total money magnet.

- I am grateful for what I have and for all that I receive.

- I have more than I need.

- Money now comes to me from unexpected sources and I am grateful.

- My income is constantly growing.

- I have the power to attract money.

- I receive money happily.

- Money flows to me easily.

- I am sensible with money and manage it wisely.

- I allow my income to constantly expand and I always live in comfort and joy.

Alright, I get it; some of that sounds totally 'woo-woo' and really isn't your style. You finally think I've lost my mind and you'll never say an affirmation as long as you live. Got it! But even if you never do, I still challenge you to have a think about your beliefs around money and what lessons you are passing on. Is some of that worth thinking long and hard about, and changing?

Did some of the other tips resonate with you? Maybe the idea of managing your funds on an app on your phone could be a simple start. Perhaps having a look at a budget or spending plan, so you do get to know your numbers and what you need to cover each pay period, is somewhere to start.

Reading a bunch of great tips is interesting and maybe eye-opening, but I'm guessing you opened the book in the first place because you were hoping you'd get something out of it that you could incorporate into your financial life.

So, if you've had a think and examined your potentially limiting beliefs around money, and kicked them to the curb, what's next?

Your next step should be to get to know your numbers, if you don't already. Work out what it actually costs you each pay period to live - that is, before you wake up every morning, how much does it cost you to cover the essentials? Only when you've worked out what your personal figure is, can you truly understand if you're living within your means or not. And I mean your figure for right now. This number can and will change over time - especially as you pay off debt. Add in all the quarterly and annual bills and divide them down into each pay period. This ticks a few of the tips we've learned to far.

You may have a gut feeling about how that exercise will work out for you, but it's best to be sure. If your take-home pay each period covers your expenses, then congratulations! You're living within your means. With what's left you can then work out what's best for you. Should you pay down debt? Especially the non-tax-deductible kind? Should you start a small but regular investment or savings plan? Could you invest in some vital protection strategies? If you don't know where to start, maybe it's time you sat down with an adviser for some guidance. Hopefully, you're now a little less resistant to that idea.

If you find you aren't living within your means, however, what then? I'd love to insert some dramatic music here, but books just really don't work that way! You've got a few options, however, so don't give up. If you can rework your debt into a combined amount with a lower ongoing payment plan, that's a start. Can you start selling things you no longer use or need to bring down what's owing? Really, if those golf clubs or bike haven't been out of the garage in a couple of years, it's time to declutter. Do you need to get a part-time job for extra income for a while until things are manageable again? Can you ask for a pay rise – if you really, truly deserve one? Can you reassess your spending and 'tighten the belt' for a while, cutting out all unnecessary expenditure – just for a time until you're back on deck?

Not facing our financial issues truly doesn't make them go away and ignorance is not bliss. Whatever your financial state is now, even if you think it's pretty dismal, it will only get worse if it's not tackled. The options provided next offer more help in this area.

Where to next?

Finding a financial professional who's right for you

As much as I'd love to have you believe that I'm the perfect adviser for everyone, the truth is I'm not. And chances are you'll find plenty of advisers who you find don't work for you, and you'll find others who do.

This is a relationship of trust, so it's worth not rushing or pushing through. Take your time and get to know this person you'll be trusting with your funds. It's your money and it's worth interviewing a few different people to make sure you've found a good fit.

Knowing exactly what you'd like to achieve from the relationship is a great place to start. Ask yourself the following questions before heading to your first appointment:

- Do you want someone you can outsource decisions to, and who'll take the stress off and manage everything on your behalf?

- Do you want to learn on the way and be actively coached to take a more pro-active role in your own affairs?

- Do you want to partner with someone who'll give you feedback on what you'd like to do and be more of a sounding board before you make decisions?

- Do you just want someone to take care of your superannuation and insurance needs?

Certain financial advisers also work with different types of clients. Many are very niched. Some specialise only in high net worth clients, for example, while others work with those in small business. Some work exclusively in the insurance field and don't touch investments or retirement planning. It's best to work out what you want before looking for the right adviser for you.

Having the internet means it's pretty easy to find out a lot more about someone before you visit. Most advisers will still tell you that their main source of referrals is word of mouth. So, ask around and pick your friends' and family's collective brains. Ask if they use an adviser, if they're happy to recommend someone and what value they feel they add to their lives. Then find out more from the internet. Most advisers will have a website, some appear on social media, offer video education or have their bio on LinkedIn. You can usually find out a lot about someone before you ever meet.

Once you've engaged an adviser, in Australia they need to provide you with their Financial Services Guide and Adviser Profile promptly. This document will outline in what areas your adviser can help, how they're remunerated, privacy consider-ations, what to do if you have a complaint and who operates as their licensee. It's actually good to read this before you engage, and most will likely have this on their website or be happy to email it out to you on request.

If you don't know where to start, industry associations often have a Find a Planner tab or link on their website, where you can search based on postcode. More recently adviser ratings has been established for Australian clients to rate their advisers and for you to find someone in your area who may have the expertise you're after.

Make sure you clearly understand all fees and charges and what value you will receive for these. And, remember, if you pay peanuts, you may get monkeys. Good financial advice is an investment you won't likely regret.

Financial things to do before you die

By now, you might have been hoping I'd get you to put together an unforgettable list of things you want to do before you die and start working out how to fund them! And truly, I do want you to make that list! Making it to Base Camp, drinking champagne at the top of the Eiffel Tower and climbing Machu Picchu are definitely up there for me!

But, unfortunately, I've also had to assist in unravelling the affairs of those who leave behind a financial mess for their family to navigate on their passing. On top of the grief, it's a bitter pill to swallow when your financial affairs have not been left 'in order'. If you've ever had to navigate estates, wills and probate, you'll know exactly what I'm talking about.

And I understand that your death is not a popular topic to ponder and is likely hard to imagine, but what if something were to happen to you? Today, tomorrow? Would your loved ones be taken care of or would they face a tough financial future? Do they know what your wishes are? Do you even have your important documents sorted?

The greatest gift you can leave your family and loved ones is having your affairs sorted out before you go. Please don't think of this as something morbid – even though it might seem like I'm backing up the hearse and asking you to smell the roses here, this isn't about you, I promise.

If you have made plans, do your loved ones know where to find them? Would they know what assets you have, what insurance policies are in place or how to access your superannuation or life insurance? Have they met your trusted advisers and know who to get in touch with if something were to happen? Have you kept them in touch with what your wishes for your estate are?

Here are some simple steps you can take to protect the important people in your life:

- consolidate your assets, if appropriate, and sort your bank accounts out

- ensure your life and personal insurances are adequate based on your current circumstances and family needs

- make sure beneficiaries have been nominated (where possible) on your superannuation or pension accounts and insurance policies (you probably don't want the ex making off with a fortune!)

- chat with your partner about what you'd like to have happen in the event of the unexpected – even hold a family council so that everyone is on the same page and knows exactly what your wishes are

- ensure your will is current – circumstances can change quickly

- arrange for an Enduring Power of Attorney or complete an Advanced Health Directive (a medical power of attorney – note that the names for these documents may differ between the states and territories in Australia)

- make sure those who need to know are aware of where your important documents are stored.

In Australia, not everything will pass through your estate, so it's wise to ensure you understand what forms estate assets and what stays outside. As an example, superannuation and homes owned as joint tenants typically are not dealt with by the will. Work through the list steadily and once it's done, make sure it's reviewed regularly. Your loved ones will be glad you did.

Wrapping up

I truly hope these stories, anecdotes and tips have been of some financial assistance to you.

If there's anything I can stress, it's to just do something. Start making small changes today in how you run your financial life. Whether it's committing to more learning, getting a spending plan started, consolidating your superannuation funds or seeing an adviser, I'd love to hear where you've chosen to begin.

Please share your journey with me on social media. I'd love to hear what steps you've made and how you're maintaining the momentum. Which idea was the number one tip that stood out to you that you thought was best to implement?

Don't let it be like those New Year's resolutions that seem like a great idea for the first three weeks of January and then fade away. This is something you need to deal with every day for the rest of your life, and ignoring it will not make it go away. Please pick the most important thing for you to do and begin.

I look forward to hearing from you and sharing in your journey along the way.

> Too many people spend money they haven't earned to buy things they don't want, to impress people that they don't like.
>
> Will Rogers

Resources and further reading

Resources and references

- Alison Hill: www.alisonhill.com.au
- Amanda Cassar: www.amandacassar.com.au
- Amy Neeson: www.amyneesonphotography.com.au
- Association of Financial Advisers: www.afa.asn.au
- Begin Bright: www.beginbright.com.au
- Business Chicks: www.businesschicks.com
- Caboodle Financial Services: www.caboodlefs.com.au
- David Batchelor, Wills & Trusts: www.wills-and-trusts.co.uk
- David Braithwaite, Citrus Financial: www.citrusfinancial.co.uk
- DB Financial: www.dbfinancial.co.uk
- Doug Bennett: www.dougbennett.co.uk
- Emma Isaacs: www.emmaisaacs.com
- Families in Transition: www.familiesintransition.com.au
- Female Excellence in Advice: www.afafemaleadvice.com
- Financial Planning Association: www.fpa.com.au
- Gwinganna Lifestyle Retreat: www.gwinganna.com
- Hands Across the Water: handsacrossthewater.org.au
- Hamlin Fistula Ethiopia: www.hamlin.org.au
- Jenny Brown, JBS Financial: www.jbsfinancial.com.au
- Ladder 87 Company: www.ladder87company.com

- Lea Schodel: www.leaschodel.com
- Michelle Hoskin: www.standardsinternational.co.uk
- Million Dollar Round Table: www.mdrt.org
- Money Habitudes: www.moneyhabitudes.com
- MoneySoft: www.moneysoft.com.au
- Peter Baines, OAM: www.peterbaines.com
- Pragmatic Thinking: www.pragmaticthinking.com
- ProBlogger: www.problogger.com
- Self Managed Super Fund Association: www.smsfassociation.com
- Solidus: www.siep.co.uk
- Soulful Experiences: www.soulfulexperiences.com
- Strategic Coach: www.strategiccoach.com
- Tanya Targett: www.tanyatargett.com
- The Hunger Project Australia: www.thp.org.au
- The Mindful Wealth Movement: www.themindfulwealthmovement.com
- Tina Tower: www.tinatower.com
- Trusted Aged Care Services: www.trustedagedcare.com.au
- Vistage: www.vistage.co.uk
- Wealth Planning Partners: www.wealthplanningpartners.com.au
- Winning Publicity Formula: www.winningpublicityformula.com
- Xero: www.xero.com
- Zaptitude: www.zaptitude.me

Recommended reading list

Baines, Peter	– *Hands Across the Water* – *Doing Good by Doing Good*
Bertrand, John	– *Born to Win*
Burke, Cathy	– *Unlikely Leaders*
Classon, George	– *The Richest Man in Babylon*
Diamantidis, Peita	– *Finance Action Hero: Basic Training* – *Finance Action Hero: Mission Possible*
Hill, Alison, Hill, Darren, and Richardson, Sean	– *Dealing with the Tough Stuff*
Hill, Alison	– *Stand Out*
Katie, Byron	– *The Little Book: Work of Byron Katie* – *Loving What Is*
Kiyosaki, Kim	– *It's Rising Time!* – *Rich Woman*
Kiyosaki, Robert	– *Cashflow Quadrant* – *Rich Dad, Poor Dad*
Orman, Suze	– *Women & Money* – *The Road to Wealth* – *The Money Class*
Rohn, John	– *The Art of Exceptional Living* – *Leading an Inspired Life* – *7 Strategies for Wealth & Happiness*
Robbins, Anthony	– *Awaken the Giant Within* – *Money: Master the Game*

Schwartz, David	– *The Magic of Thinking Big*
Stanley, Thomas J	– *The Millionaire Next Door* – *The Millionaire Mind*
Twist, Lynne	– *The Soul of Money*
Waterman, Robert H & Peters, Tom J	– *In Search of Excellence*

Check out the apps!

- Acorns
- MoneyBrilliant
- MYOB
- My Prosperity
- Xero